PENGUINS, PUFFINS, AND AUKS

A PHOTOGRAPHIC STUDY OF THE NORTH AMERICAN AND ANTARCTIC SPECIES

Penguins, Puffins, and Auks
Their Lives and Behavior

TEXT BY WILLIAM ASHWORTH
PHOTOGRAPHS AND DRAWINGS BY

Art Wolfe

CROWN PUBLISHERS, INC.
NEW YORK

Published by Crown Publishers, Inc.
201 East 50th Street, New York, New York 10022.
Member of the Crown Publishing Group. Random
House, Inc. New York, Toronto, London, Sydney,
Auckland

CROWN is a trademark of Crown Publishers, Inc.

Manufactured in Japan

Design by Lauren Dong

Library of Congress Cataloging-in-Publication Data
Ashworth, William, 1942–
    Penguins, puffins, and auks: their lives and
behavior: a photographic study of the North
American and Antarctic species/text by William
Ashworth: photographs by Art Wolfe.—1st ed.
        p.   cm.
    Includes index.
    1. Penguins.   2. Alcidae—North
America.   3. Penguins—Pictorial
works.   4. Alcidae—North America—Pictorial
works.   I. Wolfe, Art.   II. Title.
QL696.S473A84   1993
598′.33—dc20   91-32742
                                    CIP

ISBN 0-517-57551-5

10 9 8 7 6 5 4 3 2 1

First Edition

Contents

Acknowledgments

From the autumn of 1910 to the spring of 1913, an English explorer and scientist with the unlikely name of Appsley Cherry-Gerrard found himself in Antarctica as part of the support crew for the ill-fated polar expedition of Sir Robert Falcon Scott. Nearly a decade later, in 1922, Cherry-Gerrard published a book, *The Worst Journey in the World,* which captures in simple, unforgettable prose the Antarctica of the early expeditions. Here is part of his entry for June 19, 1911:

> We blundered along until we got into a great cul-de-sac which probably formed the end of the two ridges, where they butted on to the sea-ice. On all sides rose great walls of battered ice with steep snow-slopes in the middle, where we slithered about and blundered into crevasses. To the left rose the huge cliff of Cape Crozier, but we could not tell whether there were not two or three pressure ridges between us and it, and though we tried at least four ways, there was no possibility of getting forward.
>
> And then we heard the emperors calling.
>
> Their cries came to us from the sea-ice we could not see, but which must have been a chaotic quarter of a mile away. They came echoing back from the cliffs, as we stood helpless and tantalized. We listened and realized that there was nothing for it but to return, for the little light which now came in the middle of the day was going fast, and to be caught in absolute darkness there was a horrible idea.

Opposite: A thick-billed murre, a tufted puffin, and a parakeet auklet share a tiny ledge in the Pribilof Islands, Alaska.

Opposite: During the height of spring and summer, the sun never sets on Antarctica. In the golden glow of the 0230 sun, two emperor penguin adults hover over their twelve-week-old chick.

Pages xii–xiii: A pair of juvenile gentoo penguins explore lichen-covered rocks on South Georgia Island.

Pages xiv–xv: Two Atlantic puffins perch in a tree on a small island in Witless Bay, Newfoundland, Canada.

Cherry-Gerrard lived until 1959—long enough to see the astounding transformation brought to Antarctic travel by the airplane, the radio, and especially the internal-combustion engine. Today, one does not need to be an explorer to visit the ends of the earth. To obtain the striking images of Antarctic penguins that grace these pages, Art Wolfe rode to the White Continent on a tourist ship of the Linblad Line. To gain my own firsthand experience with these birds, I did not even have to go that far. My visits to the "Antarctic" took place in the Penguin Encounter exhibit of San Diego's Sea World Oceanarium, where I was allowed access to the inside of the immense, ice-filled exhibit enclosure, to walk freely among the birds and feel, for a little while, a faint echo of what it must be like on the wild ice at the bottom of the world. I am profoundly grateful to the Sea World staff —and in particular, to Melissa Barringer— for making this ersatz but strikingly realistic encounter with Antarctica possible.

Many others contributed to the success of this book, only a few of whom it is possible to thank here. David Ainley of the Point Reyes Bird Observatory north of San Francisco—one of the country's leading authorities on both penguins and alcids— granted me an excellent, pithy, insightful spur-of-the-moment interview, and even though I was making him late for a dental appointment (and come to think of it, I'm not sure which one of us should be more grateful to the other). Craig Willcox of the Point Defiance Zoo in Tacoma, Washington, and Gary Ballew of the Seattle Aquarium gave me the benefit of their hard-won practical experience handling these birds. Jean Van Tatenhove of Channel Islands National Park and Anthony R. DeGange of the Pacific Seabird Group provided ornithological contacts; Van Tatenhove also shared some of her knowledge of the Xantu's Murrelet colonies in the Channel Islands. Logistic support was provided by Hugh and Dana Small of San Diego and by my three sets of in-laws in the Seattle area: Chuck and Etta Marie James, Gordon and Harriet James, and especially Larry and Dolores James. My wife, Melody, provided, as usual, not only a great deal of much-needed moral support but the solid scientific background that her degree in biology and career in medical technology give her, and which mine—in music, writing, and librarianship—sadly lack. Finally, I would like to thank Max Gartenberg—outstanding literary agent, fine Scrabble player, and great and good friend—for bringing Art and me together on this project in the first place. Thanks, Max, I hope the product lives up in some small way to your expectations.

1

The Birds That Walk Like Us

Opposite: In their nearest approach to aerial flight, Adélie penguins leap from the ice near the Trinity Peninsula, Antarctica.

We think of birds as harbingers of spring, so we are always surprised when we come across the penguins. On the perpetual ice fields of Antarctica they frolic like children, sliding on the snow, porpoising through the frigid waters, arguing continuously at the tops of their raucous voices over patches of ice and bits of carefully hoarded stone. Always there is the cold. The birds ignore it. One species, the Adélie, spends the period of its molt—the most vulnerable time in any bird's life—crouched on icebergs in the middle of the Antarctic seas: another, the emperor, hatches its eggs and broods its young in the frigid, blustery darkness of the Antarctic winter. So striking are these images, and so thoroughly are they drilled into us by travelers' tales and television specials, that it comes as a shock to most people to discover that penguins are not, as a rule, any more polar creatures than we are: they are principally birds of the southern temperate zone, clustering around the shores of New Zealand and South Africa and southern South America, and one species is actually tropical, living and breeding directly on the equator in the Galápagos Islands.

There are no penguins in the Northern Hemisphere; here, their place is taken by auks (or alcids, as they are also referred to). A large and diverse family that includes puffins, guillemots, murres, murrelets, and auklets, the auks share a number of characteristics with the penguins, including vivid black-and-white coloration; large, densely packed nesting colonies; and the habit of pursuing fish and small invertebrates underwater, using their wings to propel themselves as if they were flying through the air. Most striking of all, the majority of auks share with the penguins the upright stance and the waddling, shuffling gait that makes us

The strong visual resemblance of these common murres to the Adélie penguins seen on page xvi is no accident, but is a result of the two species' closely similar ecological roles.

Opposite: Quick, which hemisphere are you in? Common murres, China Poot Bay, Alaska (*above*); Snares Island penguins, Snares Island, New Zealand (*below*).

think of clowns in tuxedos. Penguins and auks are the birds that walk like us, small caricatures of humans in evening dress; so strong is their resemblance to that cartoon image and to each other that it is somewhat startling to learn—as scientists have long suspected and DNA studies have recently confirmed—that the two families are completely unrelated to each other. It is lifestyle, not genetics, that has shaped their similarities. Form, as engineers and ecologists have both come to realize, follows function.

It is the ocean that is the key. The world ocean—a single immense body of water, though subdivided by geography and humans' limited imaginations into a number of separately named regions—is warm at the equator and gets increasingly colder toward the poles, a simple and intuitively obvious scheme that is made considerably more complicated by winds, currents, ice, undersea topography, and the presence or absence of various islands and continental

landmasses. Since cold water holds more dissolved oxygen than warm water does, it follows that the polar seas have a greater capacity for supporting life than do the tropical seas. Add to this the fact that poleward waters also have more nutrients in them than tropical waters—largely because the nutrients of tropical landmasses tend to be tied up in vegetation, making them unavailable to be swept to sea by rivers—and you create the potential for an enormous explosion of life in the cold waters of the far northern and far southern seas. It is not too surprising under these circumstances to find that some normally land-based creatures—birds among them—should turn to the sea as a place to live. It is cold water that is the defining factor of the penguins' and auks' life-style. Even the tropical Galápagos penguins are no exception to this: the Galápagos Islands lie directly in the path of the Humboldt Current, sweeping up the coast of South America from the cold Patagonian

Penguins are found all over the Southern Hemisphere. These Galápagos penguins inhabit the Galápagos Islands, just below the equator in the Pacific Ocean, off Ecuador.

Preceding page: A crowded king penguin rookery at South Georgia Island.

seas, and the waters around them are considerably cooler than they are elsewhere along the equator.

To go to sea, a bird must make certain adaptations. The feathers, for example, must become waterproof, or at least waterproofable. This need is met by the enlargement of a specialized gland, the uropygial, or "preening," gland, which secretes a waterproofing oil that the bird spreads over its feathers in the course of preening. Even waterproofed feathers have little insulating ability beneath the surface of the water, so to protect against cold while it is immersed the bird must develop a thick layer of fat just under its skin. The rib cage must be strengthened to resist being collapsed by water pressure as the bird dives. Feet, to be useful in the water, must develop webbing.

To these adaptations, common to all pelagic (oceangoing) birds, the penguins and

auks add a few twists of their own. To operate efficiently underwater, the wings have become short and narrow—a trend carried to extremes in the penguins, which no longer use their wings for flying through the air and so have been able to convert them to flipperlike appendages that no longer bear much resemblance to wings at all. The refractive index of water is much greater than that of air, altering the behavior of light in relation to lenses, so the birds' eyes have compensated by developing a flat, relatively stiff lens, which leaves them hopelessly nearsighted out of the water. The characteristic color pattern shown by both families, white on the chest and belly and black on the back, has developed principally as camouflage: the black back is invisible from above against the dark depths of the sea, while the light belly is invisible from below against the bright skylight on the water's surface, so the bird to all intents and purposes disappears when it dives. Finally, the upright stance of these birds on land is a direct result of their aquatic life-style. They steer with their feet while swimming, and as a consequence the feet have been moved to the rear of the body, where they can function more efficiently as rudders. Again, this has developed further in the penguins than in the auks; since they still fly, the auks must use their feet as landing gear as well as rudders, with their position on the birds' bodies something of a compromise. Like most compromises, it is not fully satisfactory. Auks hold their bodies at an awkward, steeply canted angle while standing. The uncompromising penguins walk bolt upright.

Humans have always been fascinated by penguins and auks. From the myths of the Maori and the ritualistic use of puffin bills by North American Indians right to the comic strips and television wildlife specials of today, we have found ourselves by turns bemused, awed, entertained, enlightened, and made envious by these birds that walk like us. But there has been a darker side to our relationship as well. Through the long centuries of our association we have used these birds for food, rendered them for oil, and hunted them in masses—for their pelts, for their eggs, for their meat, and too often just for fun. During the great age of European expansion, from the sixteenth through the eighteenth centuries, whole islands of birds were driven onto ships and slaughtered for use as provisions, a practice that was at least partly responsible for the extinction of the great auk—the only flightless auk species of historic times. Ten immense iron "digesters" stand today on Macquarie Island, south of New Zealand, in which between 1890 and 1920 some 5 million royal and king penguins were boiled down—some while still alive—by a New Zealand entrepreneur who was after the pint or so

Overleaf: Monolithic icebergs, which are calved from antarctic glaciers during the summer, usually remain locked in the frozen ice shelves that surround the southern-most continent. A large colony of emperor penguins is located at the base of one such iceberg at the terminus of the Dawson-Lambton Glacier. Antarctica.

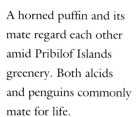

A horned puffin and its mate regard each other amid Pribilof Islands greenery. Both alcids and penguins commonly mate for life.

of oil he could obtain form each bird. The island of St. Kilda, off the coast of Britain —today uninhabited—was once the setting for a human community whose economy was based almost completely on the exploitation of members of the auk family, principally murres, razorbills, and puffins; the rockhopper penguin serves a similar function today in the economy of Tristan da Cunha in the South Atlantic. As late as 1987 there was still a cannery in Greenland operating for the purpose of preserving and exporting murre meat.

The principal threat to the auk and penguin families today, however, is not economic exploitation of the birds themselves but exploitation of other resources. Commercial fishing with vast drift nets has not only reduced the fish populations of some of the areas where these birds traditionally feed, but has caught and drowned large numbers of individual birds: a recent, precipitous 80 percent decline in the breeding colonies of murres in the Farallon Islands, off the California coast, has been attributed

directly to drift-net fishing. This population collapse took barely six years, from 1983 to 1989. The clear-cutting of timber threatens extinction for the yellow-eyed penguin along the coast of New Zealand as it does the ecologically similar marbled and ancient murrelets along the coast of northwestern North America. All of these depend for breeding on the presence of sufficient expanses of old-growth forests. Most depressing of all, perhaps, is ocean pollution, especially that resulting from spilled petroleum. Penguins and auks, as diving birds, are particularly susceptible to the effects of oil slicks, which are a major threat to the survival of the murre populations of Alaska and the British Isles, and of the jackass penguin populations of South Africa—all areas of heavy tanker traffic.

Economic development and—perhaps to a surprising degree—tourist promotions are extending these threats to the Adélie and emperor penguin populations of the Antarctic. In January 1989, the Argentine cruise ship *Bahía Paraíso* ran aground off

Opposite: Preening is an especially important activity for seabirds, which must keep their feathers well oiled and waterproof to remain afloat. This chinstrap penguin was photographed at Anvers Island, Antarctica.

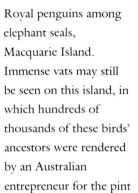

Royal penguins among elephant seals, Macquarie Island. Immense vats may still be seen on this island, in which hundreds of thousands of these birds' ancestors were rendered by an Australian entrepreneur for the pint or so of oil contained in their bodies.

A group of alert Adélie penguins checks out the scene on Paulet Island, off the coast of the Antarctic Peninsula.

Opposite: The yellow-eyed penguin, or hoiho, is the most endangered of all penguin species. Enderby Island, New Zealand.

cruise ship *Bahía Paraíso* ran aground off Antarctica's Palmer Peninsula, spilling some 170,000 gallons of fuel oil; this was just the most widely publicized of a number of similar incidents occurring in this area before and since, including the grounding of the Peruvian research ship *Humboldt*, the bulldozing of part of an Adélie rookery in the process of building an airport for a French scientific station, and the accidental release of more than 50,000 gallons of oil from a U.S. supply bunker onto the ice at McMurdo Sound.

The very fact that these incidents are being reported, however, gives us some reason for hope. If no one cared about the lives of these birds, there would be no reason to report their deaths. Caring, we can perhaps do something. It would be a pity if we did not, for certainly something necessary will have gone out of the world if the penguins and the auks leave it, something necessary not just for the health of the ecosystem but for the health of the human spirit. There is a need to know that we are not alone on this miraculous planet. The penguins and auks provide a stirring answer to this need. They stand before us, wild and awkward and strong and comic and touchingly beautiful, and we know that the salvation of the birds that walk like us is ultimately our own salvation as well.

Chinstrap penguins
decorate an iceberg off
Elephant Island,
Antarctica.

2
PENGUINS

Penguins are birds of the southern oceans —which means all oceans south of the equator, not just those near the South Pole. They are pelagic, meaning that they spend most of their lives at sea, rarely coming ashore except to breed. Their distribution as a family can be mapped quite accurately if you have data on ocean temperatures. In waters warmer than 20°C (68°F) you are not likely to find penguins; in waters cooler than that, you are. The principal exception to this rule is the Galápagos penguin, which inhabits waters along the equator that average about 23°C (73°F)—a bit warmer than most penguins like, but considerably cooler than other equatorial waters, which commonly top 28°C (82°F).

There are sixteen recognized species of penguins—or perhaps as many as eighteen. It depends on whom you are talking to. These sixteen (or eighteen) species are strongly alike, differing from each other principally in size, in bill shape, and in minor details of their external markings. All are round, compact birds, with large heads perched on short—in some cases, nearly nonexistent—necks. Their feather coats are short-vaned and dense, giving them much of the appearance of fur rather than feathers; their legs are short as well, and end in stubby little three-toed feet. All are relatively large. The smallest, the little blue, is about the length and body mass of a medium-size gull, while the largest, the emperor, stands well over 1 meter (39 inches) or more high and has an average weight of around 30 kilograms (66 pounds)—about the size of a moderately large dog. Individual emperors have been recorded with weights as high as 46 kilograms (102 pounds), which is an enormous weight for a bird, and larger than some adult humans.

Opposite: Unlike other penguin species, the emperor penguin nests on shelf ice. The young chicks must be able to care for themselves by late spring, when the sea ice breaks up. Antarctica.

An iceberg full of Adélies drifts through the waters off the Antarctic Peninsula.

Overleaf: A rookery of rare Snares Island penguins crowds the edge of a watercourse on Snares Island, New Zealand.

The most striking thing about penguins is undoubtedly their wings, which are unlike the wings of any other bird and, indeed, unlike much of anything else in the animal kingdom. They have been compared to the flippers of seals and walruses, and are sometimes called flippers, but the comparison is not fully apt. Seals' flippers have evolved from legs, and they are still used much as legs are, pulling the animal through the water with the sort of scooping motion made by the hands of human swimmers. Penguins' wings are still wings, and they are still used for flight. The difference between them and the wings of other birds is that they are designed to fly through the water.

Water is a much denser medium than air is, and the wings of penguins have undergone a number of alterations to allow them to operate efficiently there. They are shorter, and conspicuously narrower, than other birds' wings, and their cross-section profile is flatter. The elbow and wrist joints are fused and immobile, and the movement of the shoulder is limited, so that the bird must hang its wings by its sides rather than

Also known as the fairy penguin, the little blue is the smallest living member of the penguin family. Phillip Island, Australia.

Despite their heavy musculature, penguins' wings are far too small to support the birds in the air—although this gentoo on Antarctica's Wiencke Island appears to be trying.

Opposite: The wings of this resting king penguin, like those of all penguins, have no flight feathers, South Georgia Island.

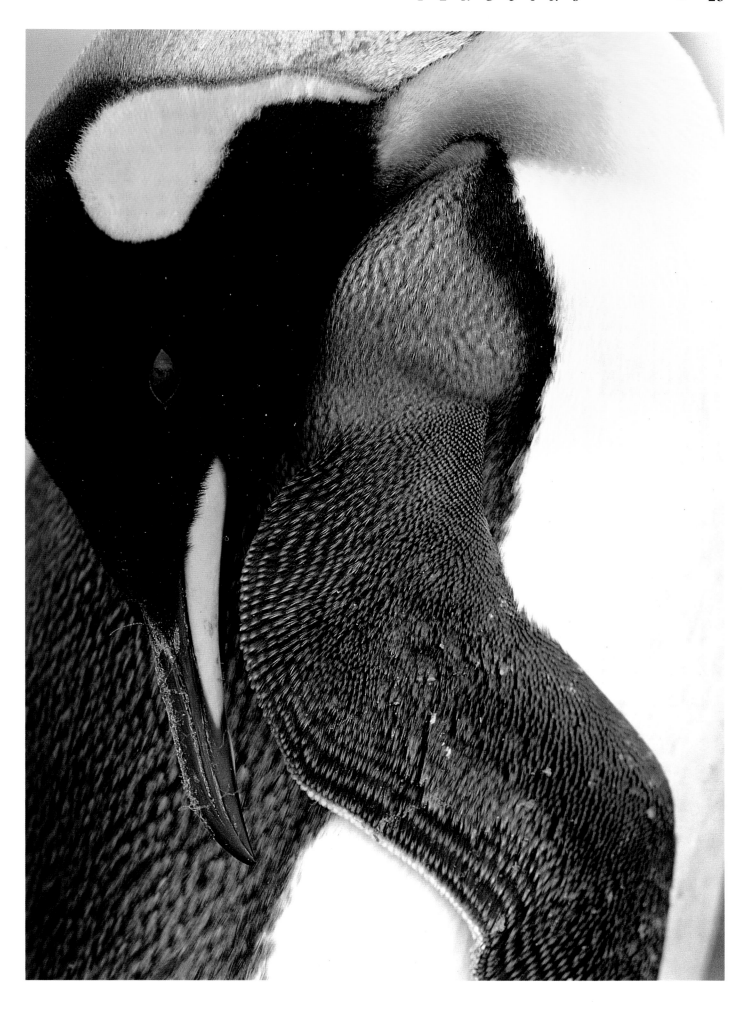

Porpoising is practiced by penguins of all species. This Adélie may have been using it to escape a pursuing leopard seal.

Right: King penguins off South Georgia Island show the typical low swimming profile of their family.

folding them over its back when it is at rest —a position that emphasizes the wings' strong visual resemblance to human arms. Flight feathers are entirely absent; the wing is covered instead with small, stiff, densely packed, and overlapping contour feathers that look like the scales of a fish. Power for forward propulsion comes from the up-stroke instead of the expected downstroke —an oddity which probably correlates with the fact that penguins are lighter than the medium they fly through, and must exert a sort of "reverse lift" designed to keep them down, instead of up, while flying.

The fact that penguins fly through the water, and do not just paddle, is easily con-firmed by a glance at their skeletal structure and musculature. Flying birds are the most specialized of all invertebrates. To provide support for the wings, their backbones have been fused into nearly rigid rods; to anchor the large muscles needed to move those wings, and to keep the center of gravity low in the body, their breastbones have been provided with an immense, jutting, blade-shape addition to the sternum known as the *keel*. Truly flightless birds such as the ostrich and the emu have lost their keels, or at best have only rudimentary ones. Penguins' keels are large and solid. The wing muscles of flightless birds are small and weak, and are composed almost exclusively of white mus-cle fibers, which are too poorly oxygenated for sustained use; the wing muscles of pen-guins are composed of red muscle fibers, and are among the largest and most power-ful muscles found on any bird. A full-grown emperor penguin is quite capable of breaking human leg bones with a blow of its wing.

On land, penguins move awkwardly, with a waddling, shuffling gait reminiscent of humans in leg irons; they are so poorly adapted for walking that most species, when confronted with snow and ice, will flop down and "toboggan," pushing with their feet and wings and sliding along on their bellies, rather than walk at all. In the water

Opposite: An incubating Adélie rests atop its stone nest on Paulet Island, Antarctica.

Icebergs are often the safest places for Adélies to sleep.

A frozen lake on Paulet Island makes a playground for a group of Adélies.

Adult Adélies usually enter the water en masse, apparently to confuse their only serious predator, the leopard seal.

Overleaf: A broad beach on Deception Island, Antarctica, makes a good pullout spot for a flock of chinstraps.

Opposite: Chinstrap penguin, Nelson Island, Antarctica. Compare this bird's white face and black eye rings to the black face and white eye rings of the Adélie on page 26.

A juvenile chinstrap eyes the photographer from the protective embrace of one of its parents on Deception Island.

it is another story altogether. The teardrop-shape penguin body is superbly streamlined; its contours are smooth and continuously curved, and its greatest thickness comes at a point about a third of the way back from the head, a shape used by naval architects when speed is of particular importance. The powerful, rigid wings propel this streamlined body at speeds up to 18 km/hr (11 mph); the ridiculous feet, suddenly not so ridiculous, trail behind and steer, directing the bird's course with easy precision. Penguins at rest, or moving slowly, swim on the surface of the water with little more than their heads showing, like giant loons. Penguins in a hurry to get somewhere swim underwater to gain speed and then leap into the air, describe a short trajectory like that of a thrown missile, and plunge back underwater again. This "porpoising," as it is called, obviously gives the bird a chance to breathe while it is out of the water; but it has other purposes as well. Since momen-

tum carries an object much farther through the air than it does through the water, porpoising uses less energy than does straight-ahead swimming. It also replenishes the tiny air bubbles that cling to the bird's feathers as it dives; these bubbles significantly reduce the water's drag on the bird's body, again improving its efficiency. Finally, the birds may simply be having fun. Penguins have a well-developed sense of play, and porpoising certainly looks playful. We have no way of knowing how they actually feel while they are engaged in it, of course, but it is hard to imagine that it doesn't stir at least a semblance of the joy we would feel under the same circumstances.

As has been noted, penguins are found all over the Southern Hemisphere beyond the barrier of the 20°C isotherm—that is, where the water temperatures are 20°C (68°F) or lower. This does not mean that

Closely related to the chinstraps and the Adélies, this gentoo on Wiencke Island differs principally in its head markings and the shape and appearance of its prominent, bright orange bill.

Opposite, above: A gentoo adult and its two chicks pose for a family portrait near Port Lockroy, Wiencke Island.

Opposite, below: A group of gentoos decorates the mossy tundra on South Georgia Island.

Marching single-file across the snow, Adélie penguins approach their rookery on the Trinity Peninsula, Antarctica. Snow and ground near pygoscelid rookeries are often stained by pink excrement, owing to the birds' dietary reliance on the brightly colored Antarctic krill.

Overleaf: This trio of kings has little to fear from the southern fur seals basking nearby. Leopard seals are the only pinnipeds that regularly attack penguins.

Below: A pair of kings is a winning hand on South Georgia Island.

all penguins are found everywhere those water temperatures exist, of course—only that penguins of some sort will always be found there. Each species has its own place in the world, its own well-defined range out of which it rarely wanders; and though the ranges of two or more species may overlap, it will always be found that each type of penguin within the area of overlap pursues a slightly different life-style, so they are never in direct competition with one another. There is a well-known rule of ecology, known as Gause's Principle, which covers this: *two species may not occupy the same niche at the same time. Niche* is used here in the ecologist's sense to mean both a physical space and a role in the dynamics of the environment. Two species cannot occupy the same niche because they would then be in direct competition throughout all aspects of their lives—for nesting sites, for food, even for lookout positions from which to spot and attack the food. The spe-

cies that was better adapted to their common life-style, even if it was only marginally better adapted, would eventually drive the other species out.

The sixteen (or eighteen) penguin species thus differ from one another not just in external appearance but in range, nesting habits, and feeding behavior and choice of prey. They are grouped, according to standard scientific practice, into six genera; the characteristics of each species within a genus (*genus* is singular; *genera* is plural) are more like those of others in its genus than they are like penguins in the other five groups.

The pygoscelid penguins—members of the genus *Pygoscelis*—are the ones whose characteristics will usually spring to mind most readily when the word *penguin* is spoken. This genus includes three very similar species. The best known of these is the Adélie penguin, *Pygoscelis adeliae,* a truly Antarctic species whose range is limited to the Antarctic continent and its adjacent waters

Perched on the insulative feet of the adult emperor penguin, first the egg and then the hatched chick are protected from the extreme cold. The parent will "nest" and "shuttle" the chick about in this fashion for the first ten weeks of its life. Antarctica.

and islands, although occasional stragglers have been spotted—far from home—in the Falklands and in New Zealand. The ultimate "little guy in a tuxedo," the Adélie is white on the chin, chest, belly and legs, and on the underside of the wings; it is black everywhere else. The round black heads with their short bills resemble small bowling balls with eyes. The legs are extremely short and buried in feathers right down to the toes, which makes them appear even shorter than they are and was probably the source of the genus name (*Pygoscelid* means "rump-legged"). These birds normally stand about 70 centimeters (28 inches) tall.

The chinstrap penguin, *P. antarctica,* is slightly smaller than the Adélie and has a range that is slightly farther north; on the Antarctic continent it is limited primarily to the Palmer Peninsula, although occasional sightings have been made elsewhere on the continental margin. Despite this, it is well named, since its breeding range is entirely within the Antarctic Convergence, the upwelling of warm water that marks the northern limit of the Antarctic Ocean. In appearance it is virtually identical to the Adélie, except that its face is white from just above the eyes down. A thin black line separating the white of the face from the white of the breast and belly accounts for the bird's rather odd common name: it looks just like the chinstrap on a British policeman's helmet.

The third member of the pygoscelid trio, the gentoo or Johnny penguin (*P. papua*), lives more northerly still, touching the Antarctic continent only at the tip of the Palmer Peninsula; it is otherwise limited in its breeding range to the Falklands, the Kerguellens, the Antipodes, and other island groups ranging roughly from latitude 50° to 60° South. It averages about 81 centimeters (31 inches) tall, and looks like a large Adélie, except that its chin is black, and its bill is noticeably longer and narrower—a sign that its diet is significantly different. A splotchy white band stretches from eye to

Towering over a flock of juvenile Adélies, this adolescent emperor on Antarctica's Trinity Peninsula has not yet developed much color in its auricular patches.

Opposite: An adult emperor penguin periodically leans forward to reassure its offspring. Antarctica.

eye across the top of its head, varying considerably in width and density from individual to individual, and it is undoubtedly the resemblance of this marking to the turbans worn by Hindu men in India that gave the bird its common name (*gentoo* is British slang for "Hindu"), although this resemblance is not really very great except to someone who hasn't seen a turban for a very long time.

All pygoscelids are highly social, breeding in large, raucous colonies in which the nests—built of small pebbles—are spaced approximately one bill thrust apart. All feed primarily on krill, the tiny lobsterlike crustaceans of the genus *Euphausia* that form the basis for the food chain in cold sea waters all over the globe. All also vary this diet somewhat by occasionally capturing small fish. The gentoo's longer, sharper bill allows it to handle larger fish than the other two species are able to; the shape of the bill

indicates that it may also eat squid, although I have not seen this listed as an item in its diet. Pygoscelid excrement is usually pink, owing to the bird's high dietary reliance on krill, and the sight of a colony of these shrieking, pink-stained penguins, surrounded by ice floes and malodorous mountains of pink guano, is a spectacle that is not soon erased from the memory.

After the pygoscelids, the birds that leap to mind most easily when the word *penguin* is mentioned are undoubtedly the aptenodids—the kings and emperors, the two species that together make up the badly misnamed genus *Aptenodytes*. (*Aptenodytes* means "featherless diver," and although these birds are indeed excellent divers they are hardly featherless; in fact, they are among the most densely feathered of all living birds.) The aptenodids are large, strik-

ingly beautiful birds in whom the typical black-and-white penguin coloration is enhanced by orange or yellow on the upper chest and the sides of the head. On the emperor penguin these head markings, known as *auricular patches* because of their location near the ears, are roughly circular and occur fairly low on the head; bright orange at the rear and upper edges, they fade to pale yellow toward the front, where they are continuous with the chest markings. On the somewhat smaller king penguin the auricular patches are in the shape of upside-down teardrops, and are located toward the rear of the head, where they run all the way to the top. They are bright orange throughout, and are separated from the silvery sheen of the back and wing feathers by jet-black outlining.

The kings, which stand a little over three feet tall, have a breeding range that is almost identical to the gentoos, and are rarely ever or never seen on the Antarctic continent. The emperors, which stand nearly a foot taller than the kings and weigh up to twice as much, breed exclusively on Antarctica and its adjacent islands. Both range much more widely when not breeding: emperors have been sighted off New Zealand and Argentina, and kings are seen fairly commonly

Well protected by its parent's brooding pouch, a very young king penguin regards its brave new world.

Left: Highly gregarious, emperor penguins will huddle for warmth during harsh weather conditions. Antarctica.

Overleaf: The distended brooding pouches of these South Georgia Island kings indicate that they are incubating eggs.

A pair of rockhoppers regard the world from an appropriately rocky perch on the Falkland Islands. Rockhoppers and macaronis are the most widespread and numerous of the crested penguins (*Eudyptes*), a genus distinguished by its jaunty, punk-hairdo-style quill head crests.

off South Africa and South America and have occasionally been spotted off Australia. Both species have large heads with long, heavy, pointed bills with which they feed primarily on squid. Their child-rearing habits are unusual. Each female lays a single egg, which is incubated—not in a nest but on top of the bird's large flat feet. During incubation the egg is covered by a heavy, densely feathered flap of skin called a *brooding pouch,* which looks a little like an inverted kangaroo pocket. In the first few weeks after hatching the young birds often return to the brooding pouches of their parents for protection and warmth, and the sight of an aptenodid chick peering out

from its parent's feet, the brooding pouch wrapped around its neck like a feather boa, is one of the most endearing in nature.

If the aptenodids are the most beautiful of all penguin groups, the eudyptids are certainly the oddest looking. The five species that make up the genus *Eudyptes*—otherwise known as the crested penguins—resemble slightly discolored pygoscelids with hairdo problems. About the size and shape of an Adélie, and colored almost identically —the chief difference being the slightly grayish tints visible on the black backs and heads of the eudyptids when they are dry—

Billing macaronis, South
Georgia Island.

A jungle of kelp makes a striking setting for this rockhopper parent and child in the Falklands.

Closely related to the rockhopper, the Snares Island penguin lives only on this island and its associated islets, off the South Island of New Zealand.

Opposite: Drying their feathers immediately after coming ashore, a flock of rockhoppers maintain a discrete distance from one another, probably to allow an uninterrupted flow of air around their bodies.

they are nevertheless easily distinguishable from their pygoscelid kin. The clue lies in the crests—the clumps of stiff, brightly colored quills that stick out of either side of the eudyptids' heads like spikes. It is almost as if a group of pygoscelid teenagers had decided to shock their elders with punk hairdos.

The quills that make up these oddball crests vary from yellow to orange in color, and are arranged in patterns that are diagnostic for each species of eudyptid. The two most common species, the macaroni (*E. chrysolophus*) and the rockhopper (*E. chrysocome*), are circumpolar in distribution. The macaronis have a range almost identical to that of the gentoos, while the rockhopper range extends slightly farther north. The macaroni's crests forms a continuous band across its forehead and lies limply along the sides of its head; the rockhopper crests arises over its eyes and sticks jauntily out

from its head, giving it the appearance of a mischievous child whose hair has been affectionately rubbed up.

The other three eudyptids are confined primarily to New Zealand and the islands to the south of it. The fjordland crested penguin (*E. pachyrynchus*) looks like a subdued macaroni without the forehead band; it is found on the northwest coast of South Island, New Zealand, and in the adjacent waters westward to southeastern Australia. The erect-crested and Snares Island penguins (*E. sclateri* and *E. robustus*, respectively) strongly resemble each other, and both look like the rockhopper; the ranges of the three overlap, and they might easily be considered a single species were it not for the fact that they apparently do not, and possibly cannot, interbreed. There are minor visual differences, if one looks closely enough: slight variations in bill color, and in the color pattern of the underside of the wing, and in the extent to which the white on the chest wraps around the neck and extends up the cheeks. The crests of the Snares Island penguin are thicker and limper than those of the rockhopper; the crests of the erect-crested are, as the name implies, exceedingly dense, stiff, and brushlike.

A sixth eudyptid, the royal penguin, is recognized by some authorities: it lives principally on Macquarie Island between New Zealand and Antarctica, where its association with large colonies of kings has given it its name. Its crests are a shockingly bright orange, making it easy to separate it visually from the other crested penguins. However, it is otherwise identical to the macaroni, with which it indiscriminately interbreeds, and most ornithologists today classify it simply as a race or color phase of this latter bird.

ERECT-CRESTED PENGUIN

Pygoscelid, aptenodid, and eudyptid penguins are primarily circumpolar in distribution; they are found in concentric, overlapping bands surrounding and centered on the South Pole. The distribution of the fourth major group of penguins, the spheniscids (members of the genus *Spheniscus*), is quite different from this. There can be no circumpolar ocean distribution in the latitudes where the spheniscids are found: the southern continents get in the way. So the spheniscids' distribution is north-south instead, along the coasts of the continents.

There are four species of spheniscids, all quite like each other and quite unlike the other penguins. They are noticeably more slender than their more southerly relatives, and their bodies lean slightly forward at rest rather than being completely upright; their bills are large and blunt, and their backs and heads are dark brown rather than black. The sides of their heads show prominent white markings that resemble a letter *U* lying on its side, with the opening toward the front.

Overleaf: Hundreds of macaronis on South Georgia Island make their way toward their rookery from the distant sea.

FJORDLAND CRESTED PENGUIN

A group of macaronis on South Georgia lines up against a rock wall.

Once considered a separate species, the royal penguins of Macquarie Island are now thought to be a geographically distinct race of macaronis. The name "royal" comes from these birds' regular association with large colonies of kings.

A similar but much larger inverted *U* crosses their chests and runs down each flank—a startling effect that makes them look a little as if someone had unsuccessfully crossed a zebra with a sea gull. They nest in burrows, which they prefer to dig in soil but will, if necessary, dig in the guano deposits left by other seabirds, including their own ancestors. Spheniscid penguins eat small to medium-size fish rather than krill or squid, and it has been shown that their rather odd coloration is very effective in helping them capture their prey. They were the first type of penguin to become familiar to Europeans, and—largely for that reason—are the nominate genus for the entire penguin family, which is known as the Spheniscidae.

The most southerly of the spheniscids, the Magellanic penguin (*S. magellanicus*), is also the most numerous and was probably the progenitor of the others. About the size of an Adélie, it nests all around the tip of South America, from the Valdés Peninsula of Argentina on the east down to Tierra del Fuego and up the west coast as far as central Chile. There are also large breeding populations in the Falklands and in the Juan Fernández Islands—the latter at about 32° South latitude, roughly the Southern Hemisphere equivalent of San Diego. Magellanics have a dark neck band above the dark inverted *U* on their chests, so their white chins are separated from their white bellies by two broad dark stripes instead of one. This makes them easy to distinguish from the other three spheniscid species.

Opposite: A quizzical pair of Magellanics regard the camera in the Falkland Islands. Magellanics are the most widespread of the spheniscid penguins, and are found from northern Argentina all the way around South America to central Chile; errant individuals have been spotted as far away as New Zealand.

Magellanic penguins flock in the shallow waters off Cape Horn.

The slightly smaller Humboldt or Peruvian penguin (*S. humboldti*) breeds from central Chile—where its range overlaps with that of the Magellanic—north through Peru almost to the Ecuadorian border, just south of the equator. It lacks the neck band of the Magellanics, but otherwise strongly resembles its more numerous cousins. Fewer than 5,000 Humboldts exist today in the wild, and the species is considered endangered.

The jackass or blackfooted penguin of South Africa (*S. demersus*) is nearly identical in size and appearance to the Humboldt but almost certainly evolved separately, probably from a wandering band of Magellanics that managed to get established off the Cape of Good Hope rather than Cape Horn. (Magellanics are greater wanderers than the other spheniscids, and have turned up in some rather odd places, notably New Zealand and Rio de Janeiro). Jackass penguins have been seen from Angola all the way around to northern Mozambique, but they normally breed only from central Namibia to about Durban, South Africa. There are considerably more of these birds than there are Humboldts, but their populations have been dramatically shrinking in recent years; they too are considered endangered.

The fourth spheniscid, the little Galápagos penguin (*S. mendiculus*), lives only in the Galápagos Islands. About two-thirds the size of the others, it has lighter, somewhat indistinct markings, and resembles a Magellanic that has been put through a poorly functioning reducing photocopier. Because their home is on the equator, Galápagos penguins regularly penetrate the Northern Hemisphere; usually these penetrations are only for a distance of a few kilometers, but the birds have occasionally been spotted off Panama, and a bedraggled, disoriented but very much alive Galápagos once turned up on a beach in southern California, though it is probable that it was tossed overboard from a passing ship rather than got there under its own power.

HUMBOLDT PENGUIN

Opposite: A rare albino Magellanic penguin perches at the edge of its burrow on Argentina's Valdés Peninsula, the northernmost limit of the species' range in the Atlantic.

JACKASS PENGUIN

The little Galápagos penguin lives on Ecuador's Galápagos Islands, making it the only tropical species in the penguin family. From its home on the equator it regularly penetrates short distances into the Northern Hemisphere.

Humboldt penguin. Peru. (*Photo: Frank S. Todd*)

Safety in numbers:
Magellanic chicks crowd
together for protection
on Argentina's Valdés
Peninsula.

WHITE-FLIPPERED PENGUIN

The little blue— sometimes called the fairy penguin—is a crow-size bird that ranks as the smallest member of the penguin family. This one was photographed on Phillip Island near Melbourne, Victoria, Australia.

Opposite: A side view of the little blue shows its somewhat unpenguinlike posture and appearance.

The remaining two genera of penguins are each monotypic—that is, they are represented by a single living species—and are both somewhat unpenguinlike, though in different ways.

The little blue or fairy penguin (*Eudyptula minor*) is quite small—about the size of a crow or a medium-size sea gull—and is blue-gray rather than black on its back and head. In all other ways it resembles a pre-shrunk Adélie. It lives around New Zealand and southern Australia, where its habit of coming ashore in masses each evening after a day of foraging at sea has been turned into a tourist attraction, with viewing bleachers near the most heavily used beaches. (A second *Eudyptula* species, the white-flippered penguin [*E. albosignata*] has sometimes been recognized. It is restricted to a single small region of New Zealand's South Island, and its differences from *E. minor* are so small that most ornithologists now class it as a race, or at most a subspecies, of the more common variety.)

The most endangered of all penguins is the yellow-eyed, or hoiho, found only in a small coastal strip of old-growth forest on New Zealand and a few associated islands, where it nests in burrows in the duff beneath the large old trees up to a mile or more from the sea.

Opposite, above: This yellow-eyed penguin on Enderby Island shows its species' striking head coloration.

Opposite, below: Royal penguin, Macquarie Island.

The yellow-eyed penguin, or hoiho (*Megadyptes antipodes*) is found only on New Zealand and a few of its offshore islands, where it nests—most unpenguinlike—in solitary burrows dug into the soil beneath old-growth forests a mile or more from the shore. Its pale yellow eyes are matched in color by a horizontal band of yellow around its head, making it appear to be blindfolded by a yellow bandanna. The rest of the head feathers have a yellow tinge to them as well. The hoiho is longer necked and weaker billed than the other penguins, and is commonly thought to be the living species with the closest ties to the common ancestor of the entire penguin family.

The place of origin of penguins is unknown, but New Zealand would be a good candidate. Not only is it the home of the relatively primitive hoiho, but it also has the greatest number and variety of living species (six, in three genera), and it shares with Antarctica and Australia the honor of hav-

ing the oldest known penguin fossils, dating from the late Eocene, about 45 million years ago. And if New Zealand is indeed the penguin family's ancestral home—as I believe it is—it helps explain why these birds are flightless. Flightlessness often develops on isolated islands, where there are no land-based predators that a bird must flee from. New Zealand has been isolated for a long time. The penguins have had more than 45 million years to establish and diversify themselves there, and to spread to other Southern Hemisphere island groups and to inhospitable continental shorelines—such as that of Antarctica—where there are no land predators either. Finally, the fact that this development in isolation did not—and in fact, could not—take place in the Northern Hemisphere is undoubtedly the principal reason that flightlessness did not become securely established among the penguins' Northern Hemisphere counterparts —the puffins and auks.

An iceberg off Antarctica's Elephant Island serves as the base and background for a striking abstraction of chinstrap penguins.

Preceding spread: Their backs turned protectively to the prevailing wind, a colony of kings incubates its eggs on South Georgia.

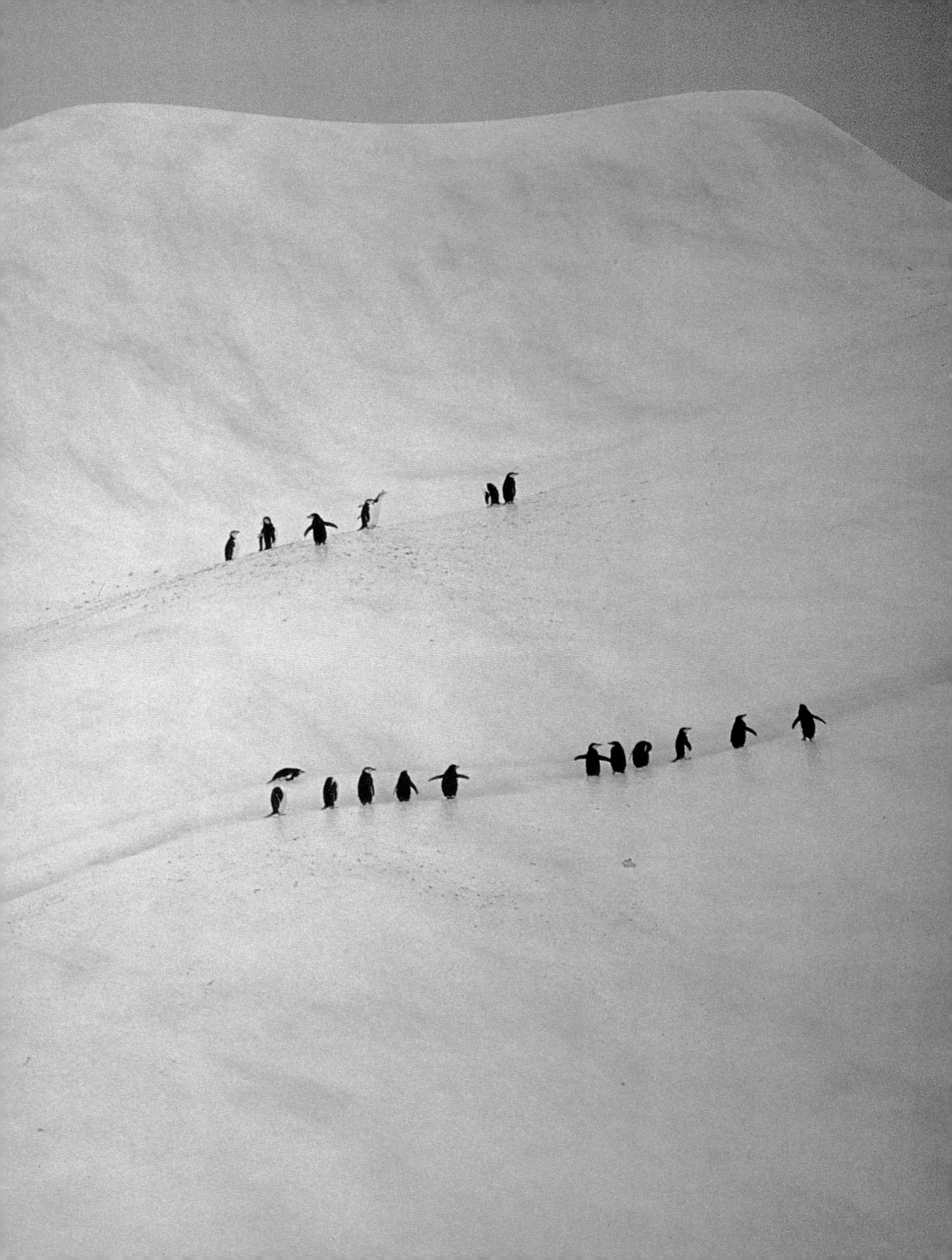

3
PUFFINS AND AUKS

The auk family (Alcidae, or alcids) includes those birds usually called auks and murres and those more commonly known as puffins. It is slightly larger in numbers than the penguin family and is considerably more diverse in character than its Southern Hemisphere counterpart, with twenty-two universally recognized species spread over thirteen genera. In appearance these birds strongly resemble the penguins, with dark (usually black) backs and light (usually white) bellies and breasts: their heads are relatively large, their necks and tails are short, and their legs are mounted so far to the rear that most must stand nearly upright on land. Like penguins, they pursue their prey underwater, steering with their feet and propelling themselves with flightlike motions of their short, narrow wings. Unlike penguins, however, all living auks can also use these wings to fly through the air. The demands of flight are the chief reason for the most obvious physical difference between auks and penguins: their widely divergent size. The largest living auk, the razorbill, is almost exactly the size of the smallest penguin, the little blue. The smallest auk, the least auklet, is not much larger than a sparrow.

Opposite: An Atlantic puffin with a beak full of capelin smelt (*Mallotus villosus*) pauses on a rock at Machias Seal Island in the Bay of Fundy, between Maine and Nova Scotia—the southernmost known breeding ground of these birds.

As with the penguins, the distribution of auk genera tends to follow ocean temperatures, with some members of the family found in nearly all Northern Hemisphere oceans where the water is cooler than 20°C (68°F); as also with the penguins, one genus is an exception to this rule, with a distribution pattern that begins where the others leave off and extends well into the tropics. Beyond these generalities, however, the distribution patterns of the two families are very different. The source of this divergence lies in the radically different geography of the two hemi-

spheres. In the Southern Hemisphere, the pole is in the middle of a continent surrounded by oceans, and in the latitudes favored by both these families of birds—20° to 50° away from the pole—ocean waters stretch uninterrupted around the globe. In the Northern Hemisphere, the pole is in the middle of an ocean surrounded by continents, and in the birds' preferred latitudes the ocean waters are chopped up into discontinuous fragments separated from each other by immense continental landmasses. Because of this, the neat, overlapping rings of concentric genera shown by the penguins could not develop in the Northern Hemisphere; instead, a confusing and muddled welter of species has arisen, each filling its own little niche in the highly varied topography. It is probably worth noting, in this connection, that flight has stayed with the alcids for the same reason that their species makeup has become so confusing: Northern Hemisphere geography. All those sea-dividing continents are full of intelligent and highly effective land-based predators. To raise their young successfully, the alcids have been forced to nest in places that are inaccessible to animals that cannot fly.

A limited amount of circumpolar seabird habitat is available, of course, on the continental coastlines that face the Arctic Ocean; and three genera of alcids have taken advantage of this and have established circumpolar distributions. Interestingly enough, these circumpolar alcids include the Northern Hemisphere birds most easily confused, in appearance, with the penguins: the murres (or guillemots) of the genus *Uria*. There are two nearly identical species in this genus: the common murre (*Uria aalge*), known in the British Isles as the common guillemot; and the thick-billed murre (*Uria lomvia*), or Brünnich's guillemot.

The common murre is a large bird with a black back and head and blindingly white underparts; it looks remarkably like a long-

Twilight in Alaska's Pribilof Islands bathes a resting pair of parakeet auklets.

Opposite: A group of common murres shares a ledge on Round Island, Alaska. The common murre—known in Great Britain as the common guillemot—is the most penguinlike of all alcids.

Overleaf: A small flock of least auklets gathers on a rock near the tide line in the Pribilofs. The least auklet is the smallest living wing-propelled diver.

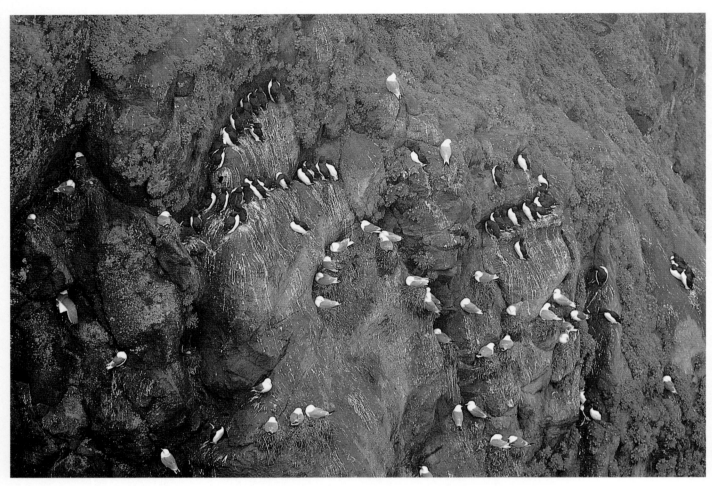

Friendly enemies: murres and red-legged kittiwakes—like all gulls, occasional predators on murre eggs and young—nest together on St. George Island in the Pribilofs.

Opposite: Common murres crowd a nesting ledge on St. George Island.

necked, long-billed Adélie penguin. Since it is among the most vertical of all the alcids, and carries its wings relatively far forward, its stance at rest does little to dispel this illusion. The most numerous nesting seabird in Britain, it is found all over the North Atlantic and North Pacific wherever its preferred nesting sites—flat-topped, vertically sided sea stacks—can be located. In the Atlantic it nests as far south as Spain; in the Pacific, a thriving colony existed until quite recently on the Farallon Islands off San Francisco, and some still live there today, although their numbers have been decimated in the last few years by drift net fishing.

The northern limits of the common murre's range extend into the Arctic Ocean above Norway and, to a lesser extent, above Alaska and Siberia. The Atlantic and Pacific populations are discontinuous, and there is some sign that they may be on their way to developing into separate species. The principal evidence for this is a color variation,

the so-called bridled morph, which appears in the Atlantic population but not in the Pacific. The bridled morph differs from the other murres principally in the presence of a white eye ring and a thin white stripe leading an inch or so horizontally back from the eye; its distribution in the population is too random and haphazard to classify it as a separate subspecies, or even as a separate race, but it seems to be more cold-tolerant than the standard color phase, and its numbers appear to be increasing. The existence of the bridled morph is probably the principal reason that Atlantic murres extend farther into the Arctic than their Pacific counterparts do.

The other *Uria*, the thick-billed murre, is slightly larger than the common murre and has a slightly heavier bill; the two species are otherwise identical in appearance and, as they often feed and nest together in mixed flocks, it can be extremely hard to tell them apart. They do not, however, appear to crossbreed. The thick-billed murre likes

Though closely related to the very penguinlike murres, the guillemots of the genus *Cepphus* bear little visual resemblance to penguins. This pigeon guillemot was photographed at Glacier Bay, Alaska.

cooler temperatures than does the common murre, so it ranges farther into the Arctic—up to the northernmost limits of land on Greenland, Franz Josef Land, and the Spitsbergen Islands—but it does not extend so far to the south. This more northerly range enables it to have a continuous distribution all around the Arctic, with no gaps over the North American and Eurasian continents, and probably as a consequence of this it has not developed clearly separable populations.

The second circumpolar alcid genus, *Cepphus,* is closely related to the *Urias* and goes by one of the same common names: its three species are known as guillemots in both Europe and North America. Only about three-fourths the size of the murres, the cepphid guillemots are identical in body outline and posture to their larger brethren, and would look just like them were it not for their coloration. Unlike all other species of auks and penguins, these guillemots are black all over in their breeding plumage. Their winter plumage is light below and dark above, like the other alcids, except that the description "dark above" must be understood here as relative: the underparts

are white, the back and head light gray. The black guillemot, or tystie (*C. grylle*), displays a conspicuous white wing patch on its otherwise all-black breeding plumage; it ranges throughout the Arctic Ocean and the North Atlantic. The pigeon guillemot (*C. columba*) replaces the black guillemot in the Bering Sea and down the Pacific coast of North America; its smaller white wing

The black guillemot replaces the pigeon guillemot in Atlantic waters. Cape St. Marys, Newfoundland.

Opposite: A thick-billed murre (Brünnich's guillemot) incubates its egg on St. George Island. The cone-shaped murre egg is laid directly on bare rock. When disturbed, it rolls in a small circle—an adaptation that helps prevent untended eggs from falling off the tiny ledges they rest on.

Pigeon guillemots gather on a sea stack in Glacier Bay, Alaska.

Opposite: Comical, graceless, and endearing, the fraterculid puffins are the best-known members of the alcid family. The horned puffin is found only in the northern Pacific.

SPECTACLED GUILLEMOT

patch is barred with black. The third cepphid, the spectacled or sooty guillemot, (*C. carbo*), is limited to the Pacific coast of Asia south of the Bering Sea. Slightly larger than the other two, it shows no wing patches and is black all over except for a white eye band, found on either side of the head, which resembles a broader, fuzzier version of the eye ring and streak found on the common murre's bridled morph.

The last of the three circumpolar auk genera—the genus *Fratercula*—is also probably the best-known alcid group of all. This is the genus that contains the "true" puffins, the Atlantic puffin and the horned puffin (puffinlike birds are also found in two other genera.) Fraterculid puffins are— the only proper word is *remarkable*—in appearance, with their bright orange legs and immense, brightly colored, comically grotesque bills. Their conspicuous black and white head markings, similar to those of the Spheniscid penguins, give them a quizzical expression, as if they were constantly faintly

amused by everything around them. Otherwise they conform to the standard auk-penguin pattern of black backs and white underparts. The Atlantic puffin, *F. arctica,* is a foot-long, football-shaped bird common throughout the North Atlantic and most of the eastern Arctic; in the winter it can be seen as far south as the Carolinas on the western side of the Atlantic and the western Mediterranean on the east. Its Pacific equivalent, the horned puffin (*F. corniculata*), ranges broadly throughout the Bering Sea and the rest of the North Pacific, squeezing into the Arctic for a short distance through the Bering Strait. It is somewhat larger than the Atlantic version (38 centimeters [15 inches] long) and carries a small "horn" of erectile tissue over each eye during breeding season; otherwise, the two species are identical. Fortunately for birders, their ranges are not contiguous, so it is possible to tell which puffin you are looking at simply by noting which ocean you happen to be in. *Fratercula,* incidentally, means "little friar," a name probably attached to the puffins because of their resemblance to a caricature of a small round man in monk's garb, though some birders insist that it comes from the bird's habit of placing its

The horned (*below*) and Atlantic (*right*) puffins are virtually identical in appearance. Note the small differences in bill color and the presence, on the horned puffin, of a small "horn" of erectile tissue over each eye. The horned puffin was photographed on the Pribilof Islands, Alaska, while the Atlantic puffin was photographed on Machias Seal Island, Maine.

feet sole-to-sole while in flight, as if clasping them in prayer.

During the last ice age (120,000–20,000 years ago) there was an ice-free area around the Bering Strait, known among paleontologists today as the Bering Refugium, to which many northern seabirds—alcids among them—retreated to escape the glaciers. This probably accounts for the confusion of alcid species found today in the Bering Sea: of the thirteen living genera, only three do not have at least one representative in this confined area of the North Pacific between the Aleutian Islands and the Bering Strait. Two of these three non–Bering Sea alcid groups, *Alca* and *Alle,* are monotypic genera found principally or exclusively in the North Atlantic: the third, *Endomychura,* is confined to the Pacific shores of North America, where it has the distinction of being the only alcid genus whose breeding range reaches into the tropics.

The sole living Alca, the razorbill (*A. torda*), is a large, heavy-bodied bird with a

tall, narrow black bill marked by white vertical grooves on either side. In posture and general silhouette it strongly resembles the *Spheniscus* penguins, though its coloring is more like the pygoscelids—or like its much closer relatives, the puffins and murres. The range of the razorbill is almost identical to that of the Atlantic puffin, although it does not get quite so far north.

The single *Alle,* the dovekie or little auk (*A. alle*), is the closest northern equivalent to the truly Antarctic penguins; its range is principally from Iceland north, although it is seen fairly commonly on the coasts of the northern United States and Europe in the winter. At sea it rarely strays far from the ice margins, following icebergs and often resting on them. It breeds on mountainside talus slopes in the high Arctic, often a considerable distance in from the sea. In coloration and body shape it is remarkably

The Atlantic puffin replaces the horned puffin in the North Atlantic. The two species' normal ranges do not intersect each other at any point.

Little auk. Greenland.
Copyright Frank Todd

A steeply slanting ledge on Alaska's St. George Island holds a few last rays of sun and a sun-seeking horned puffin.

like an Adélie penguin, but it is much smaller—averaging about 22 centimeters (10 inches), long about the size of a large jay—and is a very strong flier, able to take off directly from the water without the running start needed by most alcids. This strong flying ability, perversely, sometimes gets it into trouble: it often takes to the air under weather conditions that keep other alcids water- or land-bound, and under these circumstances can get blown far from home. Dovekies have been seen—confused, dazed, but very much alive—following storms on the Great Lakes, in Cuba, and off the coast of Africa in the Canary Islands.

The third non–Bering Sea alcid genus, *Endomychura,* contains two species, Xantus's murrelet (*Endomychura hypoleuca*) and Craveri's murrelet (*Endomychura craveri*): a third endomychurid, Scripps's murrelet, is now recognized as a subspecies of the Xantus's. These birds run 20 to 25 centimeters (9½ to 10¼ inches) in length, and resemble dovekies with white face paint. Xantus's murrelet breeds from the Channel Islands

CRAVERI'S MURRELET

XANTU'S MURRELET

off Santa Barbara, south to the Mexico-California border, and may wander south to the tip of Baja and north as far as Oregon in the off-season. Craveri's murrelet breeds exclusively at the tip of Baja and in the southern portion of the Gulf of California: the limits of its off-season wandering appear to run from about San Francisco in the north to Acapulco in the south. It is inter-

The largest living alcids, razorbills are about the size of the smallest penguins, the little blues. In appearance they closely resemble the much larger great auk, last seen alive in 1844. These birds were photographed on Machias Seal Island.

A great variety of alcids inhabit the Bering Sea, which was among the few areas of the far north to remain ice-free during the last ice age. The tufted puffin (*above*) was photographed on St. George Island, the parakeet auklet (*below*) on St. Paul Island, both part of the Pribilofs.

esting to speculate on the possibility that Craveri's murrelets might occasionally encounter Galápagos penguins far at sea, but no such meeting has been documented or appears likely to be.

The remaining seven alcid genera are all essentially birds of the Bering Sea, though most of them have established breeding populations elsewhere as well. They are a confusing, often overlapping group, with few neat divisions. Most are popularly called auklets or murrelets, but since these names follow no clear taxonomic boundaries they merely add to the confusion. Four of the seven Bering Sea genera are monotypic; two contain only two species, and one contains three. All look very much alike.

The most distinctive members of the group are the birds of the genus *Lunda*—the tufted puffins. The single species within this genus, *L. cirrhata,* is a bird about the size and shape of the horned puffin, but with an all-black body and a nearly all-white head. Its bill is standard puffin issue in dimensions and silhouette, but is not as gaudily colored as those of the "true" puffins. As if to make up for this deficiency, it carries rather bizarre facial adornments: a pair of long, pale yellow crests, one over each eye, extending jauntily back from its head and giving it a superficial but striking resemblance to the eudyptid penguins. Tufted puffins breed from California right around the Pacific to northern Japan, but their greatest concentration is in Alaska, where the population has been estimated at 4 million. They feed on a mix of krill and small fish, and when both are available they will switch back and forth, apparently because they like the varied taste. Strongly pelagic birds which are often seen far at sea in the North Pacific, they probably wander the Arctic Ocean much more than is generally realized, occasionally reaching the Atlantic.

At least one confirmed sighting has been made in Maine.

Cerorhinca, another monotypic Bering Sea genus, is also classed by ornithologists as a puffin, though it is popularly known as the rhinoceros auklet. The single species, *C. monocerata,* is slightly smaller than the tufted puffin and has a much reduced (though still sizable) bill. Its head is black, with a straggly pair of white tufts—one at the eye, another at the corner of the mouth —lying along each side. Its underparts are white. Its most conspicuous feature is its horn, which looks like a larger version of the horned puffin's eye adornment but is located in the middle of the bird's forehead, at the trailing edge of the upper mandible (the top half of bill), making it look very much like the large mammal it is named after. The rhinoceros auklet's breeding range is nearly the same as that of the tufted puffin, but the bird is not nearly so pelagic: it uses the Aleutian Islands as a bridge to

Asia and is rarely seen very far into either the Pacific or the Bering Sea. It is not known to enter the Arctic Ocean at all.

Three other Bering Sea alcid genera are made up of birds popularly known as auklets. One of these genera, *Aethia,* might be called the "true" auklets, if there could possibly be such a thing as a true auklet. The Aethids—there are three of them—are small, nondescript alcids with round heads and short, relatively heavy, bright orange bills. They live primarily in the Aleutians, ranging from there westward to Japan, and are rarely seen on the North American mainland.

Aethia cristatella, the crested auklet, is a jay-size bird with a jaunty black forward-curving crest on its forehead, giving it the appearance of a seagoing quail; it also carries a short white tuft, like that of a rhinoceros auklet, trailing back from each eye. Its back is dark gray and its chest and belly are light gray—the typical alcid-spheniscid bi-

Though its ornate bill clearly marks it as a puffin, the tufted puffin (genus *Lunda*) is otherwise very distinct in appearance from the "true" puffins of the genus *Fratercula.* Tufted puffins nest from the Bering Sea south along the Pacific coast all the way to northern California. Great wanderers, they are occasionally seen as far away as Maine.

Classed with the puffins by most ornithologists, the rhinoceros auklet breeds from the Aleutian Islands to northern California. Note the single erectile "horn" at the base of this auklet's heavy bill.

coloration—but the two colors fade into each other without a clear line of demarcation, and at a glance the bird may appear to be of a single color.

The whiskered auklet (*A. pygmaea*) strongly resembles the crested auklet but is much smaller—about 18 centimeters (7 inches) long—and has three prominent white facial crests, instead of one, on each side of its head. Its forehead crest is also much smaller.

The third aethid, the least auklet (*A. pusilla*), is the smallest alcid of all—15 centimeters (just under six inches) in length, about the size of a song sparrow. Its shape and general coloration are much like the other members of its genus, but it lacks head and facial crests altogether and has a streaked, sparrowlike breast rather than the others' solid light gray underpart coloration. Only the tip of its bill is orange.

All three of these birds feed on krill. They share a common range (though the whis-

WHISKERED AUKLET

kered auklet's range is somewhat more limited than the other two) and a common preference for laying their eggs on the bare ground, without a nest, and thus appear to violate Gause's Principle (one species in one niche at one time)—until one looks closely and discovers that this apparent unity of range and behavior is an illusion. The least auklet takes smaller food than the other two: the whiskered auklet and the crested auklet take the same size food, but hunt it at different depths. The least auklet lays its eggs on scree slopes (hillsides of small rock particles); the crested auklet lays its eggs among talus (large rock fragments); and the whiskered auklet makes its home on ledges near the tops of vertical, usually overhanging, cliffs. Each bird thus occupies a slightly

but significantly different niche. Gause's Principle, though seemingly threatened, is superbly upheld.

Closely related to the aethids is the monotypic genus *Cyclorrhynchus*. The single member of this genus, the parakeet auklet (*C. psittacula*), is about the same size as the crested auklet, but lacks a forehead crest (there are two small eye crests) and has a larger, gaudier, almost puffinlike bill. Its coloration is murrelike, with a black back and head yielding abruptly to white underparts at about the wingline. Parakeet auklets live primarily in the Bering Sea and the Gulf of Alaska—much the same range as that utilized by the aethids—and they eat the same food as the birds of their sister genus, again with slight variations in feeding depths and

In clear defiance of Bergmann's Rule, the tiny least auklet lives closer to the North Pole than all but a handful of its larger relatives.

Opposite: The crested auklet is one of several small alcids that take advantage of slightly different niches in the rich environment of the Bering Sea.

Looking very much like seagoing quail, a pair of crested auklets share a ledge in the Pribilofs with a trio of least auklets. The combined population of these two species in Alaskan waters is estimated at over 8 million.

nesting sites (in this case, crevices in bare rock slopes). They tend to wander a bit more than the "true" auklets, and have been seen as far south as the coast of Oregon.

The last of the so-called auklet genera is *Ptychoramphus*. The single species in this genus, Cassin's auklet (*P. aleuticus*), is a plump gray-and-white bird midway in size between the whiskered and crested auklets: it lacks any hint of head or facial crests, and its bill is short, narrow, and black, with just a hint of yellow along the lower mandible. Visually, it bears so little resemblance to the other auklets that there is real question why it should have this name, and some ornithologists have rebelled and begun calling it "Cassin's murrelet" instead. The species designation *aleuticus* is also a bit of a misnomer; although the bird is definitely found there, the Aleutian Islands represent the extreme northern limit of its range. The largest known breeding colonies are far to the south, on California's Farallon Islands. A plankton feeder and burrow-nester, Cassin's

auklet flies some distance out to sea each day to feed but almost always returns to the shore for the night.

The remaining four species of alcids are all known popularly as murrelets, and are all closely related, though ornithologists commonly divide them into two different genera (there must be some taxonomic reason for this, but I confess that it escapes me). All are roughly the same size—23 to 26 centimeters (9 to 10 inches) in length—and show the same general body outline, short-necked and squat, with a flat forehead and a thin, weak-looking bill. Their black-and-white winter coloration is virtually identical, and is nearly indistinguishable from the year-round coloration of their southern relatives, Xantus's and Craveri's murrelets. Their summer plumage varies, but all show, to a greater or lesser extent, a brown-and-white flecked pattern that makes them look like wrens caught in a snowstorm. None is

common, and their breeding and feeding habits remain somewhat mysterious.

The ancient murrelet (*Synthliboramphus antiquum*), like the yellow-eyed penguin, lives in burrows in the earth beneath old-growth forests: it is found all around the North Pacific from California nearly to Japan, but about half the population appears to be concentrated in the Queen Charlotte Islands off British Columbia.

The crested murrelet (*S. wumizusume*) replaces the ancient murrelet in Japan; it is distinguished, during the breeding season, by a set of short, black, rearward-leaning plumes growing from the back of its head. Its nesting habits seem to be similar to those of the ancient murrelet.

Kittlitz's murrelet (*Brachyramphus brevirostris*) lives primarily in Alaska, where it breeds on rocky mountain slopes above timberline and, at sea, often rests on ice floes. It may be thought of as the Pacific equivalent of the dovekie, though it is not nearly so common, even within its usual range.

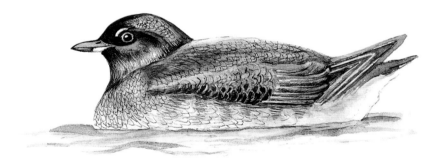

CASSIN'S AUKLET

ANCIENT MURRELET

Parakeet auklets are greater wanderers than the other small Bering Sea alcids, and are occasionally seen as far south as Oregon.

The marbled murrelet (*B. marmoratus*) is perhaps the oddest alcid of all. Though it is locally common off the Pacific coast from California through the Aleutians and clear around to Japan, and though it is often seen near dusk flying inland, no one had been able to find a breeding site until 1953, when a logger cut down a large western hemlock on one of the Queen Charlotte Islands and a somewhat startled murrelet fell out of it. It is now known that these birds lay their eggs primarily on small platforms of lichen, which they build near the bases of the large branches of old-growth conifers, usually in hemlocks and Douglas firs. This makes them the only seabirds known to nest in trees.

CRESTED MURRELET

No account of the alcids would be complete without at least a passing mention of the most famous auk of all—the great auk, or garefowl, late of the North Atlantic Ocean, extinct since June 3, 1844, when the last known living pair and the egg they were brooding were taken by pelt hunters on Eldey Island, off the south coast of Iceland. A large flightless bird roughly the size of a gentoo penguin, the great auk ranged in historic times from Great Britain around the Atlantic to Maine; in the winter it could be found as far south as Spain and North Carolina. The greatest breeding concentrations were on Funk Island and its nearby rocks, off the shore of Newfoundland. In appearance it resembled an immense razorbill, but with puffinlike white markings on the sides of its head. Its wings were tiny and totally functionless outside of the water; they also had white markings on them. Extremely awkward on land, the great auk was killed by the hundreds by sailors in search of fresh meat. Its eggs were considered delicious. It did not survive the Age of Sail.

The pathos of the great auk's extinction, and the fact that it was the only flightless auk of modern times (several others are known from fossil evidence), would be

KITTLITZ'S MURRELET

MARBLED MURRELET

enough to make it worth bringing to our attention. But there is more. It is common to call this bird the most "penguinlike" of the alcids, but that, it turns out, is getting things backward. The great auk was a penguin first. *Pengwin* was one of the most common names for the bird in English—a dialectial usage that precedes the European discovery of the Southern Hemisphere penguins by several centuries.

No one today knows just where the name originally came from. Attempts have been made to prove its derivation from the Latin *pinguis* (meaning "fat") or from the English *pin-wing* (meaning "pin-wing"), but neither case is particularly convincing. It appears most likely that the term came into English from the Welsh *pen gwynn,* meaning "white head"—an obvious reference to the great auk's facial markings and a logical means of separating it linguistically from the similar-looking but much smaller razorbill, which hunted the same waters and which, on the

scaleless face of the sea, must have been very difficult to differentiate from its larger cousin.

If the origin of the term *penguin* is obscure, however, there is no real mystery as to how it became attached to the Southern Hemisphere birds. There were plenty of Welsh sailors in the British navy. Some of them evidently sailed with Sir Francis Drake and his successors around Cape Horn, because it was during the great heyday of British exploration-with-piracy-on-the-side that the birds we know today as penguins began to be called by that name. It was a clear case of mistaken identity, but it stuck. Today the original penguin, *Pinguinis impennis,* lives on only in museum cases, while its namesakes populate the Southern Hemisphere, giving travelers in that region at least some idea of what the waters off Newfoundland must have looked like when Europeans first reached them, four hundred years and more ago.

Opposite: A group of argumentative razorbills dominates a rock outcrop on the shore of Machias Seal Island, Maine.

Parakeet auklet, St. Paul Island, Pribilofs.

Adélie penguins, iceberg
near Paulet Island,
Antarctic Peninsula.

4

A Place
in the World

In the winter the wind screams down the slopes of the Antarctic plateau, propelled by the intense cold of the continental interior. At the high center of Antarctica, air temperatures may dip to −104°C (−130°F) in midwinter, cold enough that exposed flesh freezes in seconds, rubber becomes as brittle as glass, and carbon dioxide precipitates out of the air as dry-ice "snow." As this extremely cold Antarctic air spills over the edge of the plateau and rushes seaward, pulled downward by gravity like water flowing downhill, it can easily reach speeds of over 165 km/hr (100 mph). The gales that result, known as *katabatic winds* ("gravity winds"), blow out to sea all winter, pushing the surface waters away from the coast as they go and creating powerful offshore currents that radiate outward from the continent like the spokes of a gigantic wheel.

In the summer, the katabatic winds lessen (though they are never still), but the offshore currents continue. Now the principal driving force is melting ice. Ice, even that formed from seawater, is largely salt-free, and the fresh water that results from its melting—less dense than the salt water of the seas—tends to spread out over the ocean's surface, creating a constant current northward, away from the ice.

At about latitude 50° South, the northward-flowing cold waters—now well mixed with the ocean waters and only slightly less saline than the ocean average—meet the warmer waters of the West Wind Drift, flowing endlessly around the planet between the 40th and 50th parallels. The cool Antarctic waters sink beneath the warmer waters from the north, creating a sharply delineated zone of turbulence known as the *Antarctic Convergence*. For most aquatic organisms, the steep temperature, salinity, and dissolved oxygen and nutrient gradients across the Antarctic

Opposite: A 100-foot wall of ice dwarfs the emperor penguin rookery at Dawson-Lambton Glacier. Antarctica.

Convergence create a barrier as implacable as a mountain range, and the vast differences in ecology created by this barrier justify calling the Antarctic Convergence the true edge of the Antarctic.

The water that sinks at the Antarctic Convergence must go somewhere; conversely, the water that flows away from the coast of the Antarctic continent must be replaced by water from somewhere. So the sinking water at the convergence flows southward in the middle depths of the ocean, countering the surface flow, back to the continental coastline. Here it rises in a vast upwelling fountain that brings the nutrient-enriched bottom waters—full of the organic debris that has fallen down from the upper levels of the ocean as the living organisms in these upper waters excrete or die—back to the surface again. It is this immense upwelling of bottom waters along the continental margin that makes the Antarctic Ocean one of the most productive ecosystems on earth. These intensely cold waters are brimful with life. The rising broth of nutrients supports a teeming garden of diatoms, chrysophytes, and other varieties of microscopic plantlike organisms— the phytoplankton—and these in turn support an immense population of the tiny, shrimplike crustaceans known scientifically as euphausiids and popularly as krill. The ecological term "key-industry animal" refers to the herbivore (plant eater) within a region that is the most successful in converting plant matter to animal tissue, and which therefore exists in large enough numbers to serve as the support base for a complete ecosystem of middle- and top-level carnivores, scavengers, and decomposers. On the African Serengeti, the key-industry animal is the wildebeest; on the prehistoric North American Great Plains, it was the buffalo. In Antarctica, it is the krill. These bright red, 2- to 3-cm (¾- to 1-inch) long mini-lobsters have been observed at densities approaching 17,000 to the cubic meter (13,000 to the cubic yard) in the Weddell Sea, grazing away at the phytoplankton and in turn being grazed upon—by fish, by squid, by whales, and by penguins. All Antarctic marine carnivores either eat krill or eat krilleaters. There is no other realistic choice.

At the north edge of the Antarctic, just beyond the Antarctic Convergence, the West Wind Drift flows around and around the planet, pushed by the constant westerly winds that caused the old sailing-ship crews to call these latitudes the "roaring forties" and the "furious fifties." Turbulence along the convergence maintains organic matter in suspension and keeps the water well mixed and oxygenated to a considerable depth, creating a rich ecosystem—rich enough that it is often possible to tell when you have entered the convergence because the water has taken on a greenish hue. This, however, is not the principal significance of the West Wind Drift to penguins. Its importance lies, not in its productivity or in its largely complete continuity throughout the southern oceans, but in the things that happen in those few places where it is *not* complete. Along its northern margin, the continents of South America and Africa and the southern end of the New Zealand archipelago intrude on the drift, peeling parts of it off and forcing them to become boundary currents along north-south coastlines. These boundary currents are the key to the penguins' hemisphere-wide distribution: they carry the cold southern waters far to the north, toward (and in one case, to) the equator, vastly increasing the living space available to cold-loving animals.

Along the western coast of Africa, the northern branch of the West Wind Drift is known as the Benguela Current. It bathes the shore of the continent from its tip all the way to the great bight at the mouth of the Congo, and its boundaries correspond roughly to the range of the jackass penguin.

Around New Zealand, the diverted drift currents sweep up the west coast and eddy

up to the east, joining at the top to form part of a northward-flowing open-ocean current pattern that creates a counterflow to the much warmer East Australia Current, which runs southward along the Australian coastline roughly parallel to the Great Barrier Reef. These turbulent waters, with their large variations of temperature and salinity, form homes for the richly varied penguin populations of New Zealand, Snares Island, Macquarie Island, and the others in that vicinity.

The most powerful offshoot of the West Wind Drift is the Humboldt Current (also known as the Peru Current), surging north along the rugged west coast of South America. South America sticks farther down into the drift than Africa and New Zealand do, and is therefore able to deflect more of its waters. As they flow northward along the coast, these deflected waters are augmented by a supply of frigid, nutrient-rich water from the depths of the Peruvian Trench,

brought to the surface by upwellings resulting from katabatic winds—only a little less strong than those of Antarctica—that come screaming down from the Andes. The result is a cold, powerful, organically rich stream of ocean water that brings a small touch of the Antarctic as far north as the equator, where it bathes the shores of the Galápagos Islands and allows the Galápagos penguin to survive. The ability of the Humboldt Current to support life is only a little less than that of the Antarctic Ocean itself, and the concentration of seabirds along the west coast of South America is one of the great living spectacles of the world.

The Northern Hemisphere ocean currents are different—and considerably more complicated—than those of the South. Here, there is no polar continent with its katabatic winds, no West Wind Drift, no globe-circling convergence. The predomi-

A flock of chinstraps covers a tabular berg off Nelson Island, Antarctic Peninsula. Despite their forbidding appearance, Antarctic waters are among the most prolific life zones on the planet.

Eddying up the east coast of South America, the displaced currents of the West Wind Drift bring cold Antarctic water almost to Brazil, allowing a large colony of Magellanic penguins to flourish on Argentina's Valdés Peninsula.

Opposite: King penguin, Macquarie Island.

Alaskan waters are the closest northern equivalent to the rich Antarctic Ocean. Three crested auklets, a parakeet auklet, and (*nearly hidden*) a least auklet share a temporary roost on St. George Island in the middle of the Bering Sea.

nant patterns are the so-called *gyres,* great circular clockwise-flowing currents that run around the coasts of the continents and along the equator like a single giant eddy in each ocean basin. The ocean water cools at it moves northward in the western limbs of these two great gyres, and warms as it moves southward in the eastern limbs. It is this temperature differential, along with the Coriolis force provided by the earth's daily spin on its axis, that provides the power to move the seas in this inconceivably massive fashion. Subdivided by the accident of discovery, the different limbs of each gyre take different names. If one begins off Florida, for example, the North Atlantic gyre is called variously the Gulf Stream (to Labrador), the North Atlantic Current or North Atlantic Drift (past Iceland and down the coast of Europe to Spain), the Canary Current (along the northwest lobe of Africa), the North Equatorial Current (to the West Indies), and the Antilles Current (back to Florida again). The North Pacific gyre begins as the Kuriosho Current just south of

Japan; it crosses to North America just below the Aleutians as the Subarctic Current, and bathes most of western North America as the California Current. Where it crosses the broadest section of the Pacific, just above the equator, it is called by the same name as its Atlantic counterpart—the North Equatorial Current—though the two currents have no physical connection and are in fact totally unrelated to each other.

As they wheel slowly in the ocean basins, the two great gyres spin off smaller gyres and side currents: the North Cape Current around the tip of Norway and along the arctic coast of Europe, the East Greenland Current between Greenland and Iceland, the Dyashio Current in the Sea of Okhotsk, the Alaska Current spinning around the shallow Gulf of Alaska like water around a bathtub drain. In the summer, the picture is complicated further by meltwaters from the Arctic ice pack, spreading out over the ice-free portion of the otherwise largely currentless Arctic Ocean, streaming down through the Bering Strait, and—as the Labrador Current—through the gap between Greenland and Labrador. Where these meltwater currents meet the northern limbs of the two great oceanic gyres, a convergence of sorts develops: in the Pacific, this Arctic Convergence parallels the Aleutian Islands, stirring up deep nutrient-rich waters from the Aleutian Trench and providing the Northern Hemisphere's best krill feast. This is undoubtedly why there are so many different varieties of auks in the Aleutians. In the Atlantic, the convergence is strongest off Newfoundland, where the cold, low-salinity Labrador Current—enriched by nutrients brought to the surface by katabatic winds off the Greenland ice cap—meets the warm, high-salinity Gulf Stream. The great Newfoundland seabird sanctuaries suggest how important this convergence is to the auk populations of the North Atlantic. A third convergence exists near the Spitsbergen Islands off the north-

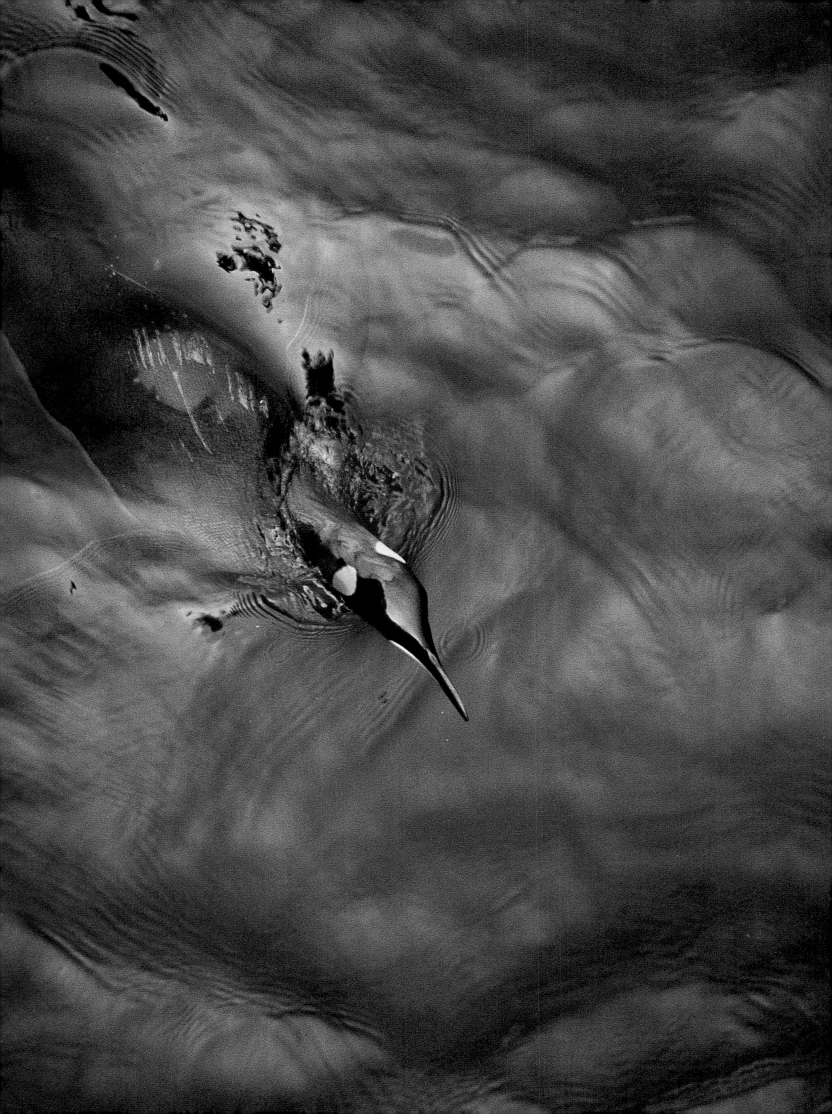

ern coast of Norway, where the North Cape Current meets the waters of the Arctic, making these islands and the nearby archipelago of Franz Josef Land—the northernmost islands of Europe—prolific areas for alcid breeding.

The greatest alcid breeding ground of all, however, is probably the Gulf of Alaska. There is no convergence here, but the currents are strong, the waters are relatively shallow, and the encircling lands are cold and wet and covered with lush, abundant rain forests, which grow slowly enough that minerals recycled from dead plants and animals are not used up but are available to be washed down the rivers and into the sea. River mouths and melting glaciers, and the unsettled mix of cold Bering Sea and warm North Pacific gyre waters that feed into the gulf on the Alaska Current, provide a wide range of temperature and salinity; highly localized katabatic winds keep the waters well mixed and the nutrients stirred up from the bottom. The result is a seabird paradise,

with plenty of good breeding habitat and an astounding variety of marine prey species that reflect the entire spectrum of salt and temperature tolerance. The birds take full advantage of the opportunities. In the Gulf of Alaska it is rare to see a rock, a patch of ocean, or even a stretch of air without also seeing a group of birds.

❧

The beauty and abundance of the cold, transparent waters where the auks and penguins make their homes always profoundly impresses humans who enter the birds' world beneath the surface. "The water below me sparkles with planktonic creatures, yet lateral visibility is fully 600 feet, the best I have seen in any waters," exulted diver Bill Curtsinger in the April 1986 *National Geographic*. Diving in the seas off Antarctica, Curtsinger had happily found himself in the middle of a community of sea creatures "as populous as that of any coral reef I have seen"—though the dive he was

Overlapping but distinct niches allow these gentoo and king penguins to coexist peaceably on South Georgia Island. Gentoos feed primarily on krill; kings, on squid and small fish.

❧

Opposite: Similar niches in the Northern and Southern Hemispheres have bred strikingly similar birds. Gentoo penguins, Port Lockroy, Antarctic Peninsula; (*overleaf*) razorbills and Atlantic puffins, Machias Seal Island, Maine.

Unquestionably the most handsome of all penguin chicks, a young emperor penguin sits contentedly atop its parent's feet. Antarctica.

describing had taken place *under* the Antarctic ice pack in McMurdo Sound. In the open water away from the ice pack, conditions can be even more impressive. Light penetrates deep into these transparent waters, allowing phytoplankton—like plants, dependent on sunlight for photosynthesis—space to bloom over a large vertical range. Feeding on the phytoplankton, and on each other, are an astounding variety of animals, primarily invertebrates: sponges and jellyfish and amphipods and the ever-present krill. Schools of small, silvery fish dart by; whales and walruses lumber past like underwater buses. In the midst of this exuberance of life, flicking about with the dynamic agility of submarine swallows, are the birds. Despite the briefness of their forays beneath the surface—though there are exceptions, most alcids and penguins can stay underwater no longer than a well-conditioned human diver, the maximum

time for nearly all species being under two minutes—the birds appear as perfectly at home as robins on a courthouse lawn, as at home as the undersea creatures they are pursuing. The majority of their dives are shallow, a few meters deep at most, but again there are exceptions: emperor penguins wearing depth recorders have reached depths of 265 meters (870 feet), and the crested auklet—one of the smaller alcids—occasionally dives deep enough to be captured and eaten by bottom-feeding fish such as groupers and cod, whose stomachs, cut open on fishing vessels, sometimes contain feathers.

In a place with an overwhelming abundance of marine life such as the Gulf of Alaska or McMurdo Sound, several species of wing-propelled divers may live and hunt in close proximity in apparent violation of Gause's Principle (one niche, one species). Closer attention, however, always reveals that the law is not violated; the niches have merely multiplied. On the Palmer Peninsula of Antarctica, for example, all three species of pygoscelid penguins—the Adélies, the chinstraps, and the gentoos—may be found breeding in the same areas, often in mixed rookeries. All three feed primarily on krill. Each species, however, takes a slightly different part of the krill population. The gentoos are almost exclusively inshore hunters, seldom ranging farther than ten kilometers (about six miles) to sea. The chinstraps forage considerably farther out—up to 150 kilometers (90 miles) from the coastline—and within that range they concentrate on adult krill. The Adélies' hunting range overlaps that of the chinstraps, but extends even farther to sea, and these birds avoid competition with their smaller but more pugnacious cousins by taking primarily juveniles, leaving the adults to the chinstraps. Thus what appears at first glance to be a single life-style proves to encompass three similar but entirely distinct niches. Abundance breeds diversity, and diversity allows subtle niche differentiation to develop.

In the North Atlantic, the puffin and the razorbill compete for the same prey in the same places: the larger razorbills will sometimes chase puffins that have been successful hunters and bully the food away from them. Again, however, there is a significant variation in the niches occupied by the two species. In this case, breeding habitat makes the difference. The razorbills breed on rock ledges; the puffins dig burrows in the sandy soil on top of sea stacks or seaside cliffs. As long as enough food remains for both species, no real niche competition exists.

Sometimes the overabundance of food in these prolific regions can lead to extreme niche specialization. The whiskered auklet, for example, shares its limited range in the Aleutians with at least eleven other alcid species with strongly similar food and shelter requirements. It avoids competition by

Puffins' serrated bills and tongues allow them to carry small fish securely crosswise. This Atlantic puffin on Machias Seal Island is holding at least four smelt; the birds commonly carry as many as seven.

feeding almost exclusively on plankton caught in the standing waves that form in the currents around sea stacks during the incoming and outgoing tides—a resource that, because of the specialized hunting skills required, is largely ignored by other birds.

If a niche gets overcrowded—that is, if a species grows in numbers to the point that the niche it occupies can no longer support all the individuals trying to utilize it—some individuals on the fringe of the population may attempt to colonize other niches near their own (*near,* in an ecological sense, means similar in character, not necessarily geographically adjacent). If the colonizers are successful, the characteristics of their offspring are likely to change slowly through the years as they adapt to the conditions of the new niche, until eventually a new species emerges. This process, known as *adaptive radiation,* is one of the principal means nature utilizes to form new species. It should therefore come as no surprise to find that, in a closely related family such as the alcids or the spheniscids, the characteristics that set one species apart from another are very often those that help it function best in the particular life-style it has evolved.

A good example of this is size. There is a rule of thumb in ecology, known as Bergmann's Rule, which may be stated succinctly as *the colder the climate, the larger the organism.* The reasons for this have to do with heat conservation. As an object increases in size, its surface area increases more slowly than does its mass, so its surface-to-mass ratio—the most important factor in the speed of heat radiation—becomes smaller and smaller, and the proportional heat loss suffered by the object becomes smaller with it. This is an obvious advantage if the object in question happens to be a bird trying to keep warm in a cold climate. Bergmann's Rule does not always hold—the smallest of the wing-propelled divers,

the tiny least auklet, lives closer to the North Pole than all but a handful of its larger relatives—but its effects can be clearly seen in most of the auk and penguin genera. Emperor penguins, for example—the most southerly of all bird species, breeding in the Antarctic winter as little as 900 miles from the South Pole—are much larger than their close relatives, the kings, which occupy the considerably more temperate climate in the vicinity of the West Wind Drift. The thick-billed murre (Brünnich's guillemot), which is slightly larger than the common murre, occupies a slightly more northerly range than its smaller relative. And the *Spheniscus* penguins of South America range themselves quite neatly along the coast by size, with the Magellanics at the southern tip of the continent being the largest, the Humboldts of the west-central coast slightly smaller, and the equatorial Galápagos penguins considerably smaller—smaller, in fact, than all but one of the fifteen other living species of penguins.

Other niche-adaptive characteristics may be less obvious than size. The puffins, for example—which feed primarily on small, slender fish such as sand eels or bird herring —have serrated tongues that, together with their immense bills, allow them to hold fish securely crosswise; this enables them to carry as many as fifteen or twenty fish back to their nests at one time. (The bills are also serrated, and those who have had to force-feed medicine to puffins have not usually enjoyed the experience. "You might as well take a steak knife to yourself" says Craig Willcox of the Point Defiance Zoo in Tacoma, Washington.) The brooding pouch of the emperor penguin is an obvious adaptation to a cold climate, and the fact that the more temperate-dwelling king penguin has a brooding pouch, too, is cited by ornithologists as evidence that the kings diverged from the emperors rather than the other way around. And the unusual mottled black-and-brown breeding plumage of the two murrelets of the genus *Brachyramphus*

Opposite: The reflective surface of an iceberg provides a stunning backdrop for a lone emperor penguin.

Recognition marks help
members of a species
identify one another for
activities such as
breeding and territorial
defense. In both the
penguins and the alcids,
recognition marks are
concentrated in the
region of the head,
allowing them to be
seen easily while the
birds are swimming.
King penguins, Falkland
Islands (*top*); emperor
penguin, Antarctic
Peninsula (*above*);
swimming kings, South
Georgia Island (*right*).

—the marbled murrelet and Kittlitz's murrelet—undoubtedly has a great deal to do with their unusual breeding habits. The marbled murrelet is the only alcid that nests in trees, and its breeding plumage—similar to that of other tree-dwellers—acts as excellent camouflage in this extremely non-seabird environment. Kittlitz's murrelet, which probably diverged from a northern population of the marbled murrelet, lives where there are no trees: it has retained the mottled plumage, however, as it also serves as good camouflage on the high mountain scree slopes that this bird has adopted as alternate nesting sites to the old-growth forests it cannot find in the far-northern latitudes it occupies.

For many years, scientists puzzled over the rather odd coloration of the *Spheniscus* penguins. The black-and-white striped effect caused by the large horseshoe-shaped markings across their chests and down their flanks makes these birds stand out rather than fade into their environment, and this flies in the face of most theories of animal coloration, which have to do with blending into backgrounds; the common exception to this rule—conspicuous breeding displays to help attract a mate—does not seem to apply here, since the markings are identical on both sexes and are maintained year-round. (The bright, conspicuous bill coverings of puffins and some auklets, by contrast, are clearly breeding displays; they fall off in the winter, leaving a smaller, dull-colored bill behind.) Recent work by Rory Wilson and his colleagues at the University of Cape Town, South Africa, however, has demonstrated that the *Spheniscus* markings actually help them capture their prey. The small fish that are these penguins' preferred food travel in large schools that tend to show what is known as *polarized behavior,* in which all members of the school react in a coordinated manner. Such close-formation maneuvering makes them behave as though they were a single large organism and makes it more difficult for predators to capture individuals within the pack. The Cape Town

investigators found, however, that drawing a model marked with the striped *Spheniscus* color pattern through the water above a school of these fish would cause the school to depolarize; the fish would "flash," scattering in all directions. If the model had been a penguin, it would have found a fish in front of it no matter where it turned—a situation that would considerably have improved its hunting luck. It is obviously no fluke, the scientists pointed out, that other animals who feed on the same schools of fish—such as the striped dolphin—show the same distinct pattern of longitudinal black and white stripes.

One of the main purposes of differences among species—along with helping them

Opposite: The presence of large landmasses and their associated predators in the Northern Hemisphere has forced alcids such as the horned puffin to retain the power of flight.

This tufted puffin on St. George Island also displays its recognition marks primarily on its head.

Royal penguins on Macquarie Island thread single-file through beached elephant seals. These large pinnipeds are not predators of penguins, but they have been known to crush the birds' eggs as they move through rookeries.

Preceding spread: Inaccessible ledges on the cliffs of Cape St. Marys allow these murres to escape all but avian predators —some of which roost with them.

fit into their particular ecological niche—is to help members of a given species identify other members of the same species, for breeding, cooperative hunting, child raising, and other species-specific tasks. Markings that have this purpose are called *recognition marks*. In the penguins and auks, they are almost always concentrated in the region of the head. The reason for this is related once again to the set of niches that they fill, and should be clear to anyone who has watched them for very long. As pelagic birds, the penguins and auks spend most of their lives bobbing about on the surface of a broad sheet of water, far from land. They are relatively heavy birds for their size, and they tend to ride low in the water. Under these very common circumstances, the head is the only part of the bird that can be seen easily. So the three pygoscelids, for example—otherwise almost identical in appearance—have easily distinguishable heads: all black for the Adélies, black with a white

band across the top for the gentoos, and white chinned—with a thin black line—for the chinstraps. You can tell them apart at sea as easily as you can on land, and in fact lifting them out of the water doesn't help a bit.

As part of the oceanic food web, the place of penguins and auks in the world is defined by their role not only as predators but as prey. What eats them is as important in determining their life-style as what they eat. In some cases, it is even more important. We have already touched on an example of this. Auks fly and penguins do not because the large landmasses in the Northern Hemisphere make land-based predators a much greater threat to the auks than they are to the penguins, and the birds have had to retain their wings as an escape mechanism and as a means of getting to breeding places—such as ledges in the middle of seaward-facing cliffs—that nonflying animals cannot reach. This strategy is not of much use, of course, against other birds; so, not surprisingly, it turns out that the principal predators of both auks and penguins are mostly avian.

The list is actually relatively short. In the Antarctic, the chief predator of penguins is the south polar skua (*Catharacta maccormicki*), a large brown bird that looks like what you might expect to get if you crossed a falcon with a sea gull. Skuas (family Stercorariidae) are actually closely related to gulls, but they have falconlike wings—narrow and sharply bent at the wrist—and wield a nastily hooked upper bill that is highly raptorial in appearance. In the temperate zone they are principally kleptoparasites, living off the prey they can steal from other seabirds who have gone to the work of catching it, but in the higher latitudes of both hemispheres they turn predaceous. Too small to be much of a threat to an adult

penguin, the south polar skuas nevertheless haunt the great Antarctic rookeries in large numbers, alert for temporarily unprotected chicks and eggs. The south polar skua, incidentally, is one of the world's great wanderers. Skuas turn up fairly often along the coasts of the Northern Hemisphere continents, presenting Europeans and American birders with the opportunity to see, if not a penguin, at least a wild bird that has recently feasted on penguin.

On the Palmer Peninsula, the south polar skua is joined as a penguin predator by its close cousin, the Antarctic skua (*C. antarctica*); and by the snowy sheathbill (*Chionis alba*), an odd, crow-size bird that looks remarkably like a predatory pigeon. Relatives of the petrels and fulmars, the all-white, bald-faced sheathbills appear to be completely dependent on penguin rookeries for their livelihood; they take eggs and chicks, steal food that the adult penguins have regurgitated for their own young, and are not

An adolescent southern fur seal discovers firsthand why his kind do not normally take penguins—especially large and aggressive penguins like these kings on South Georgia Island.

above eating the penguins' droppings if nothing else is available.

Farther north, in South America, New Zealand, and Africa, the skuas decrease in importance as predators and the sheathbills disappear altogether. Here, the principal avian predators are gulls and raptors (hawks, falcons, and owls), with ibises playing a major role in the lives of the jackass penguins. Raptors may occasionally take small adults; gulls and ibises, like skuas, concentrate on the eggs and chicks.

The same pattern holds in the Northern Hemisphere, except that northern skuas are of considerably less importance than their southern relatives. For the auks, the principal avian predators are the gulls, especially the glaucous gull (*Larus hyperboreus*) and the larger and more familiar herring gull (*L. argentatus*). Like their Southern Hemisphere relatives, these gulls primarily take eggs and chicks, and clouds of them are often seen hovering about auk-filled cliffs

and sea stacks, waiting for a chance to rush in and snatch something. Raptors are also a threat, especially the two northernmost species of falcon, the gyrfalcon (*Falco rusticolus*) and the slightly smaller peregrine falcon (*F. peregrinus*). The danger these two species hold for the auks has, of course, diminished somewhat in recent years owing to the somewhat fragile nature of the falcons' relationship with their environments, which have caused their numbers to decline as human influence in their territories has become more widespread.

In the water, penguins and auks alike are hunted principally by the pinnipeds—the seals and sea lions. Like most mammalian carnivores, these aquatic mammals are opportunistic feeders and will eat nearly anything from krill on up. But at least one seems to favor a diet of seabirds: the leopard seal of Antarctica (*Hydrurga leptonyx*), which rivals the skua as the chief predator of Antarctic penguins. An intelligent, agile

Peaceful coexistence: elephant seal and Adélie penguins, Palmer Station, Antarctica.

predator that can reach a length of more than three and one-half meters (about twelve feet) and a weight of more than half a ton, the leopard seal seems to particularly prize Adélies and will lurk about under the edges of penguin-laden ice floes waiting for the birds to enter the water. The penguins, of course, know this, and the comic ballet they do on the edge of the ice while trying to avoid being the first one into the water would be one of the most amusing spectacles of the Antarctic were it not for its deadly serious overtones. Leopard seals have a rather chilling technique of grasping a bird by its feet and, with a violent head snap, jerking it completely out of its skin—certainly not among the prettier ways to die.

Penguins do not seem to fear Weddell seals (*Leptonychotes weddelli*) and will tolerate their presence on the ice and even swim near them, though the Weddells occasionally violate this trust by taking a penguin or two. Fur seals and others are a small but significant problem for the more northerly penguins, and for the auks as well. Not all of the havoc the pinnipeds cause is due to predation; Elephant seals (*Mirounga spp.*) rarely if ever eat seabirds, but they have been known to travel en masse through the birds' rookeries, crushing nests, eggs, and slow-moving chicks beneath them on their way to and from the water.

Other aquatic predators include sharks and other large predatory fish; killer whales (which often take emperor penguins, though they rarely bother with anything smaller unless they are exceedingly hungry); and the occasional dolphin or porpoise. Galápagos penguin chicks are not uncommonly taken by the large crabs that live on and about the islands.

Land predators—mammals and reptiles —are not much of a problem for adult alcids, which can fly away from them; but

Protected by vertical cliffs and churning surf, a thick-billed murre tends its single egg on St. George Island.

An emperor penguin adult basks in the relative warmth of a late-spring morning. Antarctica.

they can easily catch penguins, and they are a serious threat to the eggs and chicks of both families. They are the chief reason that all living alcids fly, and that most penguins nest either on isolated islands or in the Antarctic, where land predators do not exist. Despite the relative inaccessability of the rookery sites chosen by these birds, however, land predators manage to make a significant impact.

For penguins, the principal problem animals are snakes and lizards; the principal victims are the Australian population of little blues and South Africa's jackass penguins, both of which are often forced to nest on the mainland owing to a lack of appropriate flat islands. (They cannot, of course, get onto steep-sided sea stacks at all; that would require flight.)

For auks, mammals play a larger role. The Arctic fox and the brown bear will both swim short distances through the surf, if necessary, to reach an accessible colony of seabirds. Polar bears, which specialize in seals, will take auks when seal hunting is poor; their principal victims are dovekies and black guillemots, the most ice-loving of the alcid species.

The land-based predator with the most impact on both these families of birds, however, is undoubtedly *Homo sapiens.* Human exploitation of these birds has gone on for millennia: great auk bones have been found in Ice Age kitchen middens along the Mediterranean, and the native inhabitants of Tierra del Fuego included the eggs of Magellanic penguins as a staple in their diets long before their first contact with Europeans. On the level of subsistence hunting, human predation has probably had no greater effect than any other natural predation. Commercial exploitation, however, has been quite another matter. We will have more to say about this—and about the impact of those predators that humans have introduced into the birds' habitats—in chapter 7.

5
SHAPED FOR COLD SEAS

Sit quietly on the beach for a while near any of the great seabird rookeries of the Northern Hemisphere and watch the birds, and you will very quickly learn to pick out the different families by their styles of flight. Gulls soar and wheel, hawklike, above the breakers; ducks power past like jet aircraft; and sanderlings flit from place to place with quick, nervous wing flicks, like seagoing wrens. Cormorants and pelicans flap gracelessly by, as prehistoric as the dreams of pterodactyls. And here and there, among the soaring and the power and the flitting and the flapping, you will see an occasional rapidly moving black-and-white blur that looks remarkably as though someone has crossed a feathered football with a buzz saw. These are the alcids. So frantically are their wings beating, and so erratic is their apparent motion, that it seems a wonder they can remain airborne, and in fact they just barely can. "They are right on the edge of not being able to fly at all," says Craig Willcox of his tufted puffins at Tacoma's Point Defiance Zoo. "People usually ask if their wings have been clipped to keep them from flying. We haven't clipped them—it's just that your average puffin has about the same glide pattern as a bowling ball."

Watch those same puffins underwater, however, and a whole new appreciation for their flying ability develops. Here the birds move effortlessly, in long, graceful glides, wings extended like a hawk riding a thermal, wingtips and trailing feet minutely and continuously adjusting course. Occasional brief, powerful wing beats provide forward propulsion. The contrast between these birds' aerial flight and their underwater flight is striking, and it leaves little room for doubt about which medium they were designed for. Their shape is adapted perfectly to the cold seas

Opposite: "The glide pattern of a bowling ball": a tufted puffin rests on a ledge on St. George Island, the Pribilofs, Alaska.

in which they hunt. Aerial flight is an inconvenient and messy necessity they can turn to if they must, but that is to be resorted to only when no other means of travel will do—and who decreed that air was the only place a bird was supposed to fly, anyway?

—

Birds are the most sophisticated and specialized of all vertebrates. The demands of the avian life-style have pulled and shaped them over the years, molding their bodies and their metabolisms and their behavior, until today they are tuned to their aerial environment to a degree that few other creatures have managed to achieve. The development of the wing is only the most obvious of these adaptations; everything about a bird, from the top of its head to the soles of its feet, is built for flight.

This shows up most clearly in the skeletal structure. Bird skeletons follow the same general plan as those of the other verte-

brates: a backbone with a rib cage attached to it, a skull perched on top of it, and four limbs, arranged in pairs, attached to a shoulder girdle and pelvis at the front and back of the torso. But their proportions, their attachments to each other, and even their internal framework are completely unlike those of the rest of us. Birds' bodies must be rigid in order to maintain their aerodynamic shape and to give the wings a solid base to operate from, hence their ribs have developed horizontal spurs called *uncinate processes,* arranged so that each rib's process overlaps and rests on the rib behind it, and their vertebrae have fused into a nearly inflexible rod. Their legs are modified into landing gear, with limited movement in the hips and knees but with springy, highly flexible ankles and toes; they are mounted so that the body can be cantilevered horizontally between them. (The reason that birds' knees appear to be put on backward is that the joints we think of as their "knees" are actually their ankles. The long skinny "legs"

During the frequent snowstorms that plague the antarctic continent, the emperor penguins lay prone on the ground, facing away from the prevailing wind for protection. It is not uncommon for the accumulating snow to completely cover the bird before the storm blows over. Antarctica.

below them are really part of the feet, the part that in a human lies flat on the ground from the heel to the base of the toe. The birds' real knees are well up along the sides of their bodies, where they are hidden in the feathers.)

The forelimbs—wings—are essentially mounted upside down, so that they meet more easily in the back than in the front; the "hand" (or forepaw) is reduced to three digits, and the proportions of the whole limb are vastly different from ours. Its joint also has a great deal more freedom of movement. A bird's breastbone is massive, with a large, thick, bladelike extension—the keel—thrusting downward from it, both to serve as a counterweight while flying and to provide a point of attachment for the powerful flight muscles. (Both the downstroke and upstroke muscles of the wings are attached to the keel and are located in the bird's breast. The former operate directly; the latter are connected to the wing bones through an intricate arrangement of tendons that use holes in the shoulder girdle as pulleys.) Finally, the bones themselves—most of them, at any rate—are hollow (*pneumaticized*), an obvious weight-saving adaptation. The hollow spaces are crisscrossed with braces like airplane girders, and are connected, through a series of lightweight bladders, to the bird's lungs; these bladders not only assure that the bird will be able to equalize the air pressure within its bones to that of the outside air as it climbs or dives in the sky, but also allow it to eliminate dead-end air passages in the lungs themselves. Air flows *through* a bird's lungs rather than in and out. This assures that all of the lungs' air-exchange tissues will be constantly exposed to freshly oxygenated air, vastly increasing their efficiency.

The extreme specialization shown by the bird's skeleton extends to other parts of the animal as well. The heavy teeth and jaws of the other vertebrates have been replaced, in these creatures, by the much more light-weight structure of the bill. The eyes are immense, reflecting the great visual acuity necessary to dodge twigs and branches while flying rapidly through trees and to spot food—or predators—from high aloft; though skin hides enough of a bird's eye that we do not often realize its size, it is a fact that in most species the weight of the eyeballs, taken together, is considerably more than that of the brain. Finally, the bird's characteristic outer coverings—its feathers—in addition to serving as insulation have been radically adapted to serve the needs of flight, and in fact flight would be impossible without them. The extremely intricate musculature of the wings and tail, allowing the bird to precisely position each individual tail feather and primary for maximum effect, shows just how important these seemingly inert adornments actually are.

Perhaps surprisingly, considering their life-style, the penguins and auks do not deviate far from this basic pattern. They do, however, finesse it a great deal, and they add a few refinements that are uniquely their own.

A cursory glance at the skeletal torso of a common murre, for example, is enough to tell that you are looking at a bird, even without the presence of the head, wings, and legs: there is the heavy keel, the fused backbone, the complex pelvic and shoulder girdles, the telltale uncinate processes along the rib cage. But the proportions are off. The keel is longer and shallower than that of a nondiving bird, and is shaped into a beautifully streamlined parabolic curve; the rib cage is elongated, and the whole skeleton is narrow and graceful, so strikingly so that the skeleton of an aerial bird placed next to it looks clunky and awkward by comparison. The uncinate processes are narrow and graceful, too, and each one extends two ribs back instead of one, greatly strengthening the rib cage—an obvious ad-

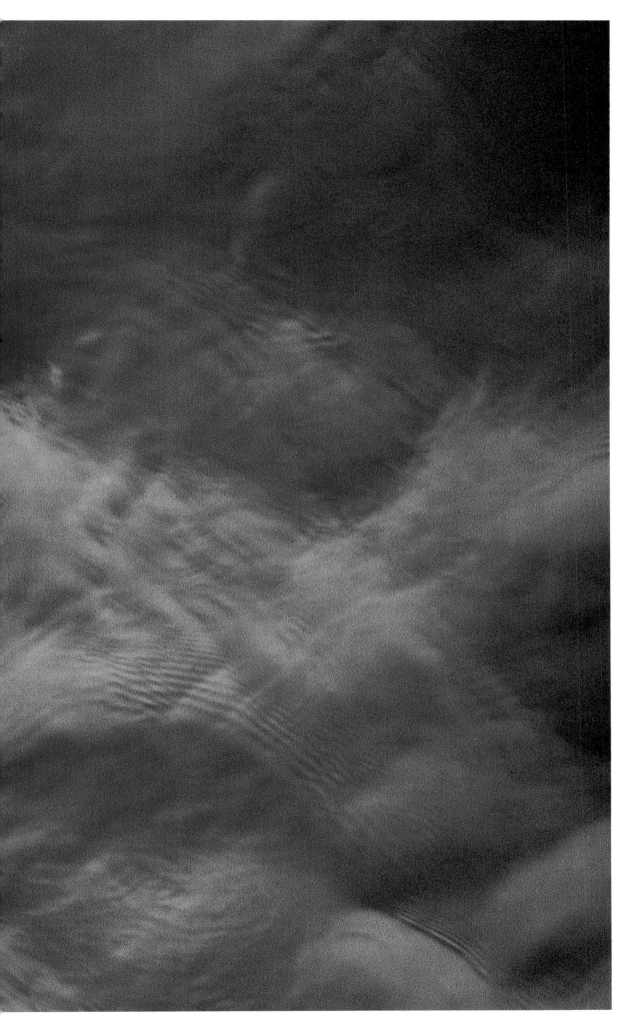

King penguin,
Macquarie Island.

aptation to deep diving that helps keep the chest from collapsing under the pressure of 100 meters or more of water. The bones are also denser and more solid than those of strictly aerial birds, with only a limited amount of pneumatization, increasing the bird's relative density and allowing it to stay underwater more easily.

The penguin torso is similar to that of the murre, only more pronounced: more streamlined, more dense, more strongly braced. Penguin skeletons show no pneumatization at all: the bones are solid clear through, like those of a mammal or reptile. (Even this does not seem to make the birds as heavy as they would like to be relative to the water. Penguins commonly swallow fairly large stones, apparently with the purpose of increasing their overall density, so that they can make themselves essentially weightless in the water and counter the common tendency to bob to the surface upon relaxation.) The penguins' uncinate processes are even sturdier than the murre's, and the whole bird shows almost perfect streamlining, rounded at both ends and with its greatest thickness coming about a third of the way back, as if it had been designed by an engineer using a wind tunnel. The extreme torsal rigidity of penguins and auks, incidentally, is one of the reasons that they must propel themselves underwater with their wings. Other aquatic vertebrates have highly flexible backbones, and are able to drive themselves through the water by undulating their bodies from side to side. Birds—being birds—cannot do this.

The wings of these birds, as we have already mentioned, are short and narrow—extremely so in the penguins, which no longer use them for flight and hence have been able to convert them entirely to flipperlike appendages, with fused wrist and elbow joints and only limited movement in the shoulder. The wing bones are flattened in the plane of the wing, increasing its

The penguin's bill and eyes remain those of its aerial ancestors. Compare this gentoo's head with that of the black guillemot on page 82.

Opposite: The tightly overlapping, scalelike feathers of a royal penguin's wing show why early sailors thought penguins might be more closely related to fish than to birds.

Opposite: Penguins'
wings, unlike those of
the alcids, have no flight
feathers. This Adélie on
Paulet Island is
protecting what at first
glance appears to be a
fuzzy rock; it is actually
a very young chick, still
in its gray infant down.

This Atlantic puffin's
wings are only
marginally larger than
those of the penguin on
the facing page.

streamlining when it is moved through the water edge-on. The legs of both groups have been moved backward to allow them to be used as rudders, although this is far more pronounced in the penguins than it is in the auks. The knees of both groups show odd forward projections—again, more pronounced in the penguins—called *cnemial crests;* these serve as attachment sites for the powerful muscles needed to adjust the legs quickly and precisely in the thick medium of water.

The most strongly characteristic bone of penguins is the foot bone, or tarsometatarsus. As in all birds, it is a single bone that originated as a fusion of the three bones found in the mid-foot region of reptiles and mammals. In all other birds—including the auks—the tarsometatarsus is long and narrow, allowing the feet to reach far forward during landing and, in the nonflying runners such as the ostrich, creating a fast, springy, ground-eating stride to escape from predators on the open plains. Penguins neither fly nor run, and their tarsometatarsi are short and thick. Functionally, this keeps the feet close to the body while serving as rudders, increasing streamlining and decreasing heat loss in the cold seas. It also creates the penguins' staunchly upright stance and contributes to the rolling, waddling gait we humans find so amusing. So unique and easily recognizable is this bone, and so unlike anything else in the animal kingdom, that its presence in a fossil deposit is enough to confirm at a glance that penguins were once present there, even if no other part of the bird is ever found.

The auks and penguins show many other physiological specialties that help shape them for the cold seas they live in. Most of these—like the skeletal adaptations—are closely parallel from one family to the other. All birds of both groups, for instance, have very large uropygial (preening) glands, in order to produce enough oil to completely waterproof their feathers during preening before and after dives. All show a layer of fat directly under the skin (*subcutenaceous fat*), which serves as insulation during dives. In the Antarctic penguins and the high Arctic alcids, which regularly brave water with a temperature of about −2.2°C (28°F)—seawater at these temperatures does not freeze because of its salt content—this fatty layer may account for as much as a third of the bird's weight.

Because they are pelagic—creatures of the open sea—penguins and auks must be able to survive for long periods of time without access to fresh water, something they accomplish by drinking seawater and excreting the excess salt by means of specialized glands in their heads. The salt is released as a thick, concentrated brine that drips out of the birds' nostrils. This so-

called salt gland is not unique to these two families, of course; all pelagic birds, and most shorebirds, excrete salt this way. When you see one of these birds vigorously shaking its head, it generally means the salt glands have been active, and the bird is trying to rid itself of the drops of brine running down its bill.

The penguin's feathers are of particular interest. Most birds, including alcids, have two principal types of feathers, *vanes* (the stiff blades we usually associate with the word *feather*) and *down* (small, fluffy undercoat feathers that serve as extra insulation next to the skin). Penguin feathers are neither: they are intermediate between the two types, with vanes at the tips and down at the bases. An extra quill, the *aftershaft,* sprouts near the base of each feather; it is entirely covered with down. Penguins are not the only birds to grow these multipurpose feathers (chickens and other gallinaceous birds are another family that have them), but they are probably the only ones

to grow them to the exclusion of everything else. The small, overlapping vanes at the tips of these feathers, especially on the wings, have a decidedly scalelike look, and they are undoubtedly the physical reason behind the myth that grew up among seventeenth-century sailors that the penguin was not a bird at all, but a fish with feet and a bill.

Not only the shape but the distribution of penguin feathers is unusual. In most birds the feathers are arranged systematically, in rows (*feather tracts*), with lines of bare skin between them. Penguins have no feather tracts; the feathers are distributed uniformly over the body. Their density and length varies according to the climate a particular penguin species lives in, with the Antarctic species (not surprisingly) being the most thickly covered. The emperor's skin may sprout as many as twelve feathers per square centimeter (77 feathers to the square inch); Adélies' feathers are no denser than that, but they are proportionately longer and they cover the entire bird, in-

Opposite: A preening Paulet Island Adélie demonstrates the use of oil from the uropygial gland to waterproof its feathers before going to sea.

The three-toed penguin feet, with their short, thick tarsometatarsal bones, are highly distinctive. King penguin, Macquarie Island.

cluding the base of the bill and all of the foot except the webbed toes themselves. Penguins, like all birds, have extremely high metabolic rates and must maintain an internal body temperature of between 38° and 39°C (roughly 100° to 102°F). It is a measure of the efficiency of feathers as insulation to note that, despite the metabolic furnace burning so fiercely just below the surface, snow that falls on a penguin's pelt does not melt—an old wives' tale that happens to be perfectly, literally true.

I have mentioned the high metabolic rates of birds. It is probably worthwhile to spend a little more time discussing that subject here.

Metabolism is the engine of life—the fire within the living cell that drives all creatures, from bacteria to humans. It is based on a slow, highly complex set of chemical reactions—the Krebs cycle—that is essentially the same throughout the living world. There are, however, a great many variations as to how this basic cycle is applied to the task of keeping an organism alive.

One important distinction is that made between *homoiothermalism* ("warm-bloodedness") and *poikilothermalism* ("cold-bloodedness"). The internal temperature of a poikilothermal organism (a lizard, an insect, a tree) approximates that of its surroundings; its metabolic processes follow these temperature differences, slowing down in cold weather and speeding up when it gets warm. A homoiothermal organism, by contrast, attempts to maintain a constant temperature regardless of its surroundings; its metabolism creates rather than follows its internal temperature.

Homoiothermal organisms are much more adaptive than poikilothermal organisms, and are able to remain active and alert through a much broader range of environmental conditions. But there is a price for this adaptability. As with a building that is heated or cooled to maintain a constant temperature, winter or summer, a ho-

moiothermal organism must be constantly expending energy for temperature control. As a consequence, its rate of metabolism must be much higher than that of a poikilothermal organism. This in turn leads to a much higher rate of fuel consumption (for fuel, read "food") and a consequent need to spend considerably more time eating and foraging. It is undoubtedly these massive energy demands that have kept homoiothermalism a relatively rare phenomenon—so rare, in fact, that only two classes of living organisms have adopted it. Mammals are one. Birds are the other.

Note the use of the phrase "temperature control" rather than "heat production" in this discussion. Staying warm in a cold environment definitely takes extra energy, but so does staying cool in a warm one. All organisms—homoiothermal and poikilothermal alike—have what is referred to as a *zone of thermoneutrality,* a range of air temperatures within which they function most efficiently. When the air is warmer or cooler than this optimum temperature zone, they must compensate in some manner. For humans, the zone of thermoneutrality seems to be at about 26°C (just under 80°F). We can afford to keep our houses and public buildings cooler than this because we wear clothing. For the tropical and temperate-zone penguins and auks, it is probably in the same general range. For the Arctic and Antarctic species, it is much lower. Adélie penguins, for instance, will begin to show symptoms of heat stress if the temperature rises much above 0°C (32°F).

Several methods are used by these birds to control their internal temperatures. Some are behavioral: crowding together to keep warm, flapping the wings and panting to keep cool, seeking the sun or the shade as appropriate. Others are physiological. The insulative value of feathers and fat is of obvious use at temperatures colder than thermoneutrality. Less obvious, perhaps, is that this insulation must be countered at warmer temperatures, *warmer* here simply meaning "above thermoneutrality." It may seem

Standing on the ice and spreading their wings, Adélie penguins attempt to keep cool off Paulet Island. Adélies are in danger of heat stroke whenever the air temperature climbs much over 0°C (32°F).

anomalous that a penguin sitting on the ice in 5°C (41°F) air should be in danger of heat stroke, but this is indeed the case. To deal with this threat, the birds use two interrelated techniques. The feathers are held in a ruffled position, exposing some skin directly to the outside air. (This is easier for the auks, whose feathers are in tracts, than it is for the penguins.) And the ability of the skin to act as a radiator is increased by opening the capillaries directly beneath it, so that more blood can pass close to the surface and be cooled. (Here the penguins have the upper hand; their fat layers have developed a complex, interwoven capillary system whose chief function appears to be to serve as a heat exchanger, precooling the blood flowing toward the skin by bringing it nearly into contact with the blood flowing back from the skin into the body.) It should be observed that both feather ruffling and blood pumping require an output of energy. Cooling down, like warming up, is an energy-intensive process.

In addition to the energy needed to maintain constant internal temperatures, homoiothermal organisms—like poikilothermal organisms—must also expend energy to move about, catch and consume food, breed, and otherwise do all the things that animals do. Here, the life-styles of penguins and auks pose special problems. In order to provide the energy used for activity, an animal's metabolism must increase: the greater the activity level, the higher the metabolic rate. Higher metabolic rates require higher oxygen consumption. We breathe harder when we run in order to get more oxygen into our bodies, and our hearts beat faster so that this extra oxygen can be carried more rapidly to the body cells that are using it up so fast. Birds have extraordinarily high metabolic rates because flight is among the most energy-consumptive tasks of all. But what happens when that flight takes place where oxygen is unavailable, beneath the surface of the planetary sea?

In fact—and despite years of intensive study—the answer to that question is not yet fully known. A great deal has been learned, but much of it seems to fly in the face of common wisdom. In birds, for example—as in humans—greater exertion normally leads to a faster heartbeat, and since powered flight requires large amounts of exertion, a bird's heart rate tends to be at its maximum during this activity. This is true of all aerial fliers, including the alcids, when they are in the air. When they fly underwater, the reverse happens: the heart slows down. On long dives, the heartbeats of both auks and penguins are reduced to 20 percent or less of their resting heartbeat on the surface. In fact, the whole metabolic process appears to slow down. No data seems to be available for auks or penguins, but for diving ducks—which show very similar reactions—metabolic activity has been proved to slow down by as much as 90 percent while they are under the water,

even if they remain physically active during this period.

One reason for this, though clearly not the only one, is that travel actually becomes easier once the bird has submerged; underwater swimming is from two to five times as efficient as swimming on the surface, and relative efficiency actually climbs as a bird's speed increases. The principal cause of this is the water's surface tension, which makes it much harder to push a body through than most people realize. The rather odd habit shown by the smaller alcids of leaping into the air before they begin a dive is a direct consequence of this. They have to literally stand back and throw themselves at the water surface to break through.

The respiration rate, of course, falls even more dramatically than the heartbeat. Far from being able to inhale more rapidly, an air-breathing animal such as a bird must stop inhaling entirely underwater, no matter how hard it is pushing itself. Where,

Like penguins, alcids make extensive use of their wings to help control their body temperatures. Horned puffin (*below*) and common murre (*overleaf*), both photographed in the Pribilof Islands, Bering Sea, Alaska.

then, does the oxygen required by metabolism come from? Common sense would say that it comes from the reservoir that is present in the lungs when the dive begins, but common sense would be wrong. In fact, these birds exhale before they dive so that their lungs will be empty, reducing the risk of nitrogen narcosis (the "bends"). Emptying the lungs also makes it easier to deal with pressure changes, since the pressures inside and outside the lungs are no longer fighting each other (the volume of air decreases approximately by half for each approximately ten meters [33 feet] of diving depth, drastically affecting a full lung's pressure balance). It also significantly reduces buoyancy, bringing the bird's overall density much nearer to that of water and making it easier to maneuver beneath the surface without having to fight a constant tendency to drift upward. Oxygen for underwater flight obviously cannot come from these empty lungs. But if not from the lungs, where?

One answer may be nowhere. The muscles of all animals are capable of limited amounts of energy production without the direct use of oxygen, a process called *anaerobic catabolism*. The procedure involved is essentially a short-circuit of the Krebs cycle. Glycolysis, the chemical reaction that drives the cycle, is tapped directly for the energy needs of the body instead, and the chemical by-products of the reaction, which would normally be fed into the cycle as raw materials, are simply put aside. This process creates an "oxygen debt" that must eventually be made up, and this oxygen debt is the reason why athletes—even well-conditioned ones—cannot go on running forever. (The buildup of one of the by-products of glycolysis, lactic acid, is a chief cause of muscle cramps.)

For a long time it was assumed that diving birds simply used a form of glycolysis-based anaerobic catabolism while they were underwater, and this may indeed be true much of the time. But suspicion arises. If

these birds depended entirely on glycolysis while flying underwater, the oxygen debt in the wing muscles would have to be immense. There is, however, no sign of any debt at all, and in fact alcids can go quite easily from flying underwater to flying in the air with no significant pause in between. The expected lactic acid buildup has apparently not occurred.

It would seem, then, that one must look elsewhere, and more and more scientists are. Current research on murres and Adélie penguins, as well as on deep-diving mammals such as seals and sea lions, seems to point to another chemical entirely: *phosphocreatine* (PCr), the complex hydrocarbon that provides the actual power for muscle contraction. In most vertebrates, PCr is produced largely as it is needed, using the energy produced by glycolysis; only a small store remains in the muscle at rest. In the air-breathing divers, however, a significant amount of PCr seems to build up in the muscles during rest on the surface, where glycolysis can go on without creating an oxygen debt. This allows the animals to shut off glycolysis completely during their dives, at least as long as the stored PCr holds out. The discovery that PCr can be synthesized at rest holds great promise for advancements in human medicine. If the process can be isolated and understood, it may help victims of muscular dystrophy, whose symptoms are produced—at least partly—by a slow deterioration of the body's ability to produce PCr.

Despite their very real advantages over fur, both as an insulating medium and as an aid to flight, feathers have one distinct disadvantage: they cannot be continuously grown, but must be replaced entirely when they become worn. This necessity gives rise to the annual plumage bedragglement we know as the *molt*. At a given time each year —usually shortly after the close of the breeding season—the old, worn feathers become loose in their sockets. The new ones

grow beneath them, pushing them out. The process cannot be comfortable, and in fact birds seen during molt almost always appear to be stolidly enduring, not enjoying themselves at all.

Most birds molt the contour feathers on their bodies all at once, getting the process out of the way as rapidly as possible; but they molt their flight feathers two at a time, one from each wing, ensuring that they will be able to continue to get off the ground. The alcids, in common with many other water birds, reverse this, molting their wing feathers all at once but only gradually replacing their body feathers. This renders them temporarily flightless, but preserves their waterproofing and thus assures that they will be able to dive. Flightnessness dur-

This king penguin's expression seems to indicate that molting is as uncomfortable as it looks.

Opposite: Stay cool, baby; an adolescent Adélie takes advantage of natural air conditioning as it molts its juvenile plumage on an iceberg off Paulet Island.

ing the molt does not appear to be a problem; the birds are through raising their young by this time and have moved out to sea, so they have no need to escape land-based predators or to fly to their breeding ledges. Some—the dovekie is one example—even begin their annual migration in the flightless state, traveling up to a thousand miles by using their swimming skills and a good push from the North Atlantic gyre.

An exception to this pattern is found in the smallest alcids—the auklets of the genus *Aethia*. These tiny diving birds, like land-based flying birds, molt their flight feathers two at a time, one from each wing. The reason for this appears to relate to their size. If they molted all their flight feathers at one time, the surface area of their wings would become too small to propel them underwater.

Penguins do not follow the alcid pattern, but molt all their contour feathers at once, like land birds. And since they have no flight feathers, this means that they molt all their feathers at once, period. During the time of the molt, which may last from two to six weeks, they lose all their waterproofing and are unable to enter the water. Since all their food comes from the water, this means that they cannot eat. They compensate by gorging themselves in the month or so before the molt, building up fat reserves that can be drawn on during their enforced fast and that will serve as extra insulation if the weather happens to turn cold during the relatively unprotected time of the molt.

During the molt itself, penguins remain as inactive as possible, conserving the energy stores that they cannot replace. It is not uncommon for travelers in the Antarctic to come upon ice floes that are pockmarked with shallow pits surrounded by rings of heaped-up feathers. Each of these pits marks a place where a penguin has stood, unmoving, for the several weeks· required to lose its old feathers and grow new ones, waiting until its plumage has become waterproof again and it can go back into the sea, the realm in which all penguins and auks most completely and beautifully belong.

Wing detail, king penguin, Macquarie Island. Unlike most birds, penguins molt the feathers from their wings and bodies simultaneously.

A pair of bedraggled
emperors suffer through
their molt at
Commonwealth Bay,
Antarctica.

Pages 152–153:
Icebergs adrift off the
Antarctic Peninsula
commonly carry flocks
of cold-adapted Adélies.

Emperor penguin
rookery at the Dawson-
Lambton Glacier.
Antarctica.

6
THRIVING ON THE EDGE

As a writer researching various topics in natural history, I often find myself in odd or unusual places. One of those places, a few years ago, was the inside of the immense Penguin Encounter exhibit at San Diego's Sea World aquarium. It was an unforgettable experience, full of wonder and interest—wonder and interest that were not limited, in any degree, to the humans in the party. Penguin curiosity is legendary, and those who venture among them discover very quickly that the legends are not exaggerated. As soon as we stepped onto the ice, my guide and I found ourselves the center of attention in a milling crowd of knee-high birds, cocking their heads from side to side, regarding us with the bright-eyed wonder of children at a circus, pecking at our pant legs to see what they were made of, clamoring for attention and—quite likely—for a better view of these freaks. One little rockhopper followed us about as we walked through the exhibit, persistently untying our shoes.

It would be easy to say that these were tame birds looking for a handout, but that would not be entirely true. The Sea World exhibit is designed to be as natural as possible; the birds are treated by the staff much as they would be if encountered in the Antarctic, and most of the feeding is done underwater. And there are strong individual variations in the birds' behavior, anyway. Outside the main exhibit at Sea World there is an open-air enclosure holding a small group of Magellanic penguins, who can take the Southern California heat better than the Antarctic varieties are able to. Most of these birds, one recent day that I visited, were going about their business and ignoring the passing crowds of people. One was not. Flat on his belly, chin on a convenient rock, one young penguin lay at the uppermost

Opposite: A Falkland Islands rockhopper penguin with a mischievous look.

Both alcids and penguins engage in the type of courtship behavior known as the ecstatic display. Razorbills, Machias Seal Island, Maine.

point of the exhibit, intently watching the people watching him. At times it was difficult to tell who was more curious about whom; we might just as well have been the exhibit and the penguin the one who had come to see.

It is generally conceded that birds are not the brightest of animals. Scientists will tell you that their behavior is largely pre-patterned and goaded primarily by instinct. They point to the small size of a bird's brain (as we have already seen, its eyeballs are usually bigger) and to the extreme stereotyping of its behavior, which, though it may be extraordinarily complex, is usually invariant in the face of a particular stimulus. Once the behavioral train leaves the station, it tends to plow forward to its destination, whether or not the destination remains appropriate. "Birds, because of their rich endowment of wings, have never been

required to develop clever brains," wrote the great American ornithologist Joel Welty a few years ago (*The Life of Birds, 2nd ed.,* 1975). "As a consequence, much of their behavior is, by mammalian standards, fragmentary, stereotyped, and, on rare occasions, amazingly stupid." The popular pejorative "bird brain" shows how well most of us agree with Dr. Welty's assessment.

To dismiss bird behavior as simple merely because it is largely instinctive, however, risks oversimplifying what is in fact an extremely complicated situation. Since birds depend so thoroughly on instincts, they are well supplied with them, and much of this broad repertoire is highly developed and complex. Often more than one instinct applies to a given situation, and the bird must make a choice—and the fact that this choice usually proceeds quickly and unconsciously does nothing to lessen the element of unpredictability it adds to the bird's behavior. It is, for example, very common to see a bird and its mate preen each other's feathers—a gesture that looks, and may be, rooted in affection, much like a human couple giving each other mutual back rubs. Such joint preening, however—known technically as *allopreening*—is also remarkably similar to territorial defense mechanisms used by many of the same birds, and it is not at all unusual to see an allopreening couple become more and more aggressive, letting the territorial behavior take hold, until the preening strokes become blows and one or the other of the partners is knocked off the branch or the nesting ledge. At that point the ferocity ceases, and when the displaced bird flies back to its perch, allopreening normally resumes as if nothing at all had happened.

And instinct doesn't explain all of bird behavior, anyway. Like all vertebrates, birds show good learning ability, both simple habituation and the more complicated variety known as *insight learning,* in which the animal must generalize from its experience, making the sort of leap of logic that says,

for example, if a bit of food was behind the red door last time, it is likely to be under the red box this time. Birds get better with practice, even at instinct-driven tasks. A young bird's nest is likely to be far less stable and well designed than those of its older relatives, and a male bird's territorial song, while retaining the instinctive outline common to its species, will almost always show individual variations that increase in complexity and interest as the bird ages. At times, a young bird's dependence on learning may extend into odd and unexpected quarters. In the back room at any zoo with an established penguin breeding program you will almost always find, among the incubators and the ice-makers and the food processors, a large open tank filled with water. It is there for what may seem to be an extremely bizarre educational purpose. These most aquatic of birds, so perfectly adapted to a life at sea that they can barely function on land, shun water as chicks and will flounder about helplessly and a little

Allopreening, in which two birds preen each other's feathers, is most commonly seen in mated pairs. Galápagos penguins, Galápagos Islands, Ecuador.

Adélie penguins lining up to ride passing ice floes look like small children waiting for a carnival ride. The game may continue for several hours.

fearfully if they are placed in it. Each young penguin must be taught, individually, how to swim.

Birds play. This may be particularly true of the penguins and auks: life on the edge means living in an environment where the elements are a constant threat, and the experimentation that is the more serious side of play is often necessary simply to remain alive. But whatever the reason, it is clear that these creatures often do things for the sheer, unbridled joy of doing them. A familiar tale from the Antarctic, for example, is the Adélie penguins' game of ride-the-ice-floe. A group of Adélies will crowd the edge of a small ice shelf, waiting for a bit of floe ice to drift by on the tidal current. When one does, the birds leap aboard and ride it along the shore for several hundred yards. At the end of the ride they leap off, scramble ashore, and toddle back to the original

jumping-off place to catch the next floe. The game may continue for hours, with lines of jostling birds forming at the jumping-off point like children waiting for a ride on the roller coaster. No scientist watching this performance has ever been able to come up with any reason for penguins to behave this way other than just for the sheer hell of it.

Or consider the common murre's game of poke-your-neighbor. Murres, in common with most alcids, assemble at sea in large flocks known as *rafts*. It is not unusual for people observing these rafts to see one of the birds suddenly leap into the air with a surprised flutter of wings, the victim of what appears to be a crude practical joke. Another murre in the flock will have quietly slipped underwater, swum directly under his unsuspecting neighbor, and come up beneath his victim with his sharp bill pointed straight up. There is, of course, a possible nonplay explanation for this: the underwater bird may simply need to clear a place to come up for air. But this does not

explain why it sometimes happens to birds with plenty of open space around them. It also does not explain a similar game described by Gary Ballew at the Seattle Aquarium. His captive murres share their enclosure with a number of other alcids, and it often happens that one of these other birds—usually a puffin—will be standing on a ledge next to the water when a murre will quietly stick its head up, grab its smaller relative by the leg, and pull it in. The victim is always immediately released, so this cannot be classed as a misapplied form of predation. The murres apparently just want a horse laugh at someone else's expense.

Murres are considered difficult to keep in captivity because they are so aggressive, chasing one another and other birds around the enclosures, poking their heads into puffin and auklet nesting burrows, and occasionally killing small shorebirds that may be placed in with them, or that wander in accidentally. Most keepers chalk this up to the birds' inherent pugnacity. Ballew disagrees.

"They're just bored," he says. "They need something to keep them occupied." His murres have been seen pulling sea urchins and other invertebrates off the walls and floor of their pool, bringing them to the surface, and playing catch with them. Ballew has tried substituting rubber balls out of compassion for the urchins; the murres accept the new toys eagerly, but they always manage to tear them to shreds within a few days.

A different aspect of these birds' intelligence figures in another story the Seattle curator likes to tell. He has tried keeping his murres behind nets. It hasn't worked. The birds have systematically gone down the edges of the nets, clipping the soft electrical ties used to hold them together, until a gap opens wide enough for them to go through. It is, of course, dangerously misleading and anthropomorphic to compare another animal's behavior to our own; but it becomes nearly impossible to avoid making this comparison when the animal in question is a

Rockhoppers on the Falklands live up to their name.

supposedly "dumb" bird who is in the process of handily outwitting you.

Play, of course, is essentially extraneous behavior. Though it may help practice skills that will be useful in other contexts, it is not itself directly necessary for survival. What can be said about these animals' "work" behavior—the behavior directly connected with food gathering, protection, shelter, and perpetuation of the species?

As it turns out, a great deal can be said about it, and much of what can be said is highly intriguing. Because these are warm-blooded creatures who have chosen to live in cold climates, and because they are representatives of those most aerial of creatures —birds—who have chosen to spend a large part of their time underwater, much of their behavior is unusual. And since a species' behavior, like its physique, is shaped at least in part by its environment, many of the unique aspects of penguin and auk behavior parallel one another. These birds do not just look alike, they act alike as well. Parallel evolution has worked on behavior as thoroughly as it has worked on anatomy.

At least one observer, David Ainley of the Point Reyes Bird Observatory near San Francisco, believes that a single environmental factor—availability of nesting sites —may explain most of the behavioral similarities between the two groups. Both penguins and alcids, he points out, are strictly limited in the number of sites they can use. Penguins, because of their inability to fly, concentrate in areas where beaches and other points of easy access to the seas are available. Alcids must limit their nesting to cliffside ledges and the summits of sea stacks, where the eggs and flightless young will be inaccessible to predators. It is from these site limitations that the intensely colonial nesting behavior common to both groups has developed. The birds must constantly interact with others of their species, and the result is a group of behavioral complexes that are both unusual and strikingly alike.

Take, for example, the matter of vocali-

zation. Both penguins and auks are highly vocal birds, and in both families the level of noise tends to rise with the density of the colony—that is, each individual bird tends to vocalize more often as the number of birds living close to it increases. Part of this is the result of the inevitable territorial squabbles that go with packing more and more individuals into the available space (any human planning board can sympathize), but much of it derives from the unexpected fact that, although they are highly visually oriented animals, most of these birds do not seem to be able to recognize their mates and offspring by sight but must depend on voice identification to tell each other apart. Individual penguins and auks apparently look as much alike to each other as they do to us, and the continual cacophony in a seabird colony is essentially one long series of "who-the-hell-are-you?" calls. Parents recognize their offspring in this manner; mates recognize each other, even after the long separation of migration; and

An alert and inquisitive tufted puffin belies the common image of birds as little better than instinct-driven machines.

Penguins and alcids both normally live in dense colonies—a circumstance that helps explain their strikingly similar behavior patterns. Chinstrap penguins, Deception Island, Antarctica (*opposite*); murres, Cape St. Marys, Newfoundland (*overleaf*).

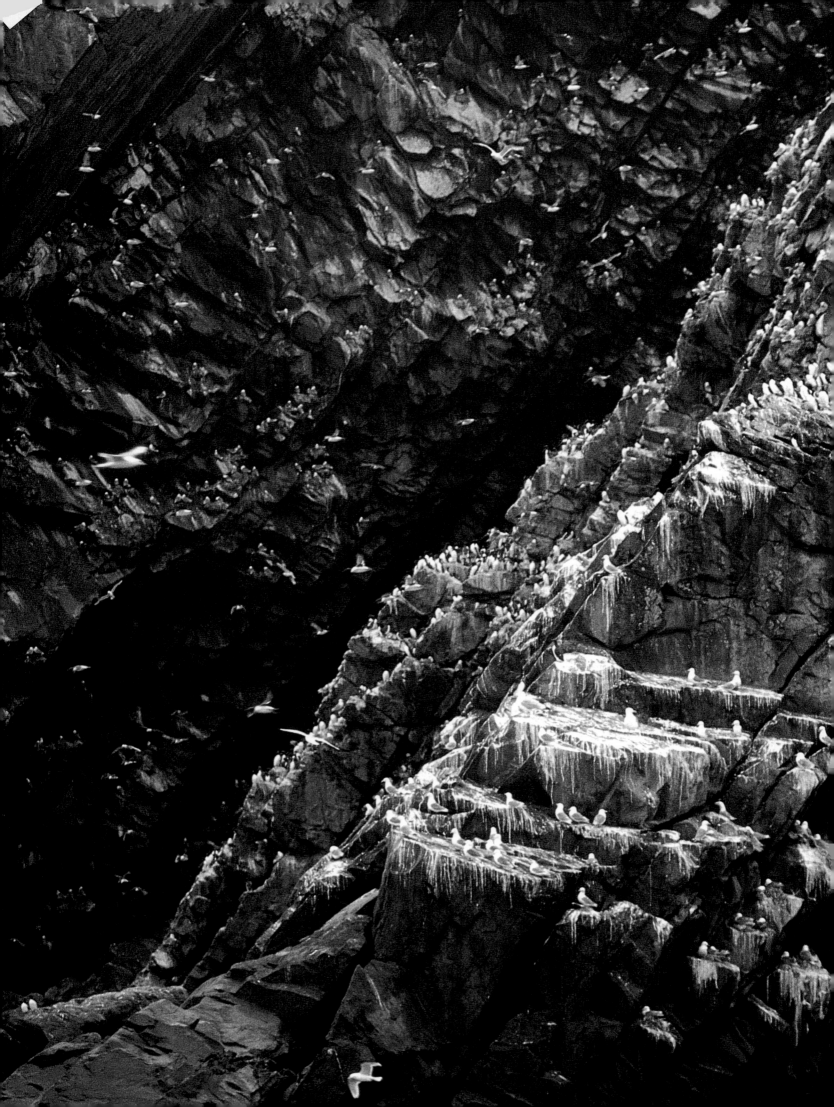

it is probable that nesting neighbors know one another's voices, allowing them to tell the difference between neighbors and intruders, tolerating the former and ganging up on the latter.

The most remarkable vocal-recognition performance in either family is probably that put on by the ancient murrelets. These birds nest in burrows beneath old-growth conifers, generally within sight of the sea, along the northwestern coast of North America. Their young are precocial, meaning that they can move about and feed themselves very soon after hatching, but they still need parental care, partly for protection against predators and partly for education in hunting techniques and choice of food. Since this education must take place at sea, the burrows are abandoned when the chicks are only one or two days old.

Usually an entire colony will move out at once, in the dead of night. In the dark there is no hope of parents and offspring recognizing each other by sight; all must be done by voice. The parents, working together,

move partway down the slope to the sea and call the young from the burrows. The young follow, calling back. When they are satisfied that both their chicks have left the burrow, the parents fly a little ways out to sea, settle on the water's surface, and resume their calling. The chicks, who cannot fly, stumble down the slopes in the darkness, enter the ocean in a mass wave of tiny feathered bodies, and swim toward their parents' calls. In the dark, in the roar and tumble of the surf and the cacophony of frantic calls, the chicks somehow find their own parents and the parents, their own chicks. The family, reunited, swims together toward the open sea.

Pygoscelid penguins—Adélies, chinstraps, and gentoos—are also very adept at vocal recognition. Their semiprecocial young are capable of alert movement shortly after hatching, but their infant down is not waterproof, so they cannot go to sea until after their first molt. The parents must feed them until this first molt takes place,

and since each parent quite determinedly feeds only its own offspring, parent-child recognition is critical to these birds. Early in the chick's life the parents take turns going to sea, and their recognition of each other is sufficient to make sure the food they bring back gets to the right chick. As the chick grows and larger quantities of food are needed, however, both parents must forage at once. During this stage the chicks leave their nests and gather in large assemblages called *creches* (a British term for day-care centers), where their collected body heat can help one another keep warm and their sheer numbers can deter attacks by skuas. (Adults sometimes stand sentry duty over the creches, but it is usually half-hearted, and it is really not needed anyway; skuas ordinarily attack only isolated chicks.) An adult returning from the sea and approaching one of these creches will be mobbed by frantic youngsters seeking handouts. All of these plaintive pleas will be ignored except the ones coming from the

Above and opposite, below: Arguing like a pair of alley cats, two Atlantic puffins dispute a piece of the rock on the coast of Machias Seal Island. Strong territorial behavior is encouraged by colonial dwelling.

Opposite, above: Courtship or conflict? The two types of behavior are often very similar. Adélie penguins, Palmer Station, Antarctica.

A pair of rockhoppers
express their strong
feelings about each other
in the Falkland Islands.

An adult chinstrap penguin approaching a creche of juveniles will be mobbed by youngsters asking for a handout, but will feed only its own chick.

Opposite, above: The smaller of two gentoo chicks near Port Lockroy on the Antarctic Peninsula begs hopefully from its larger sibling. The young of pygoscelid penguins are on their own much of the time while both parents forage.

adult's own chick—an identification that appears, as with the ancient murrelets, to be made entirely by the sound of the voice.

Puffins are at the other extreme. They are burrow dwellers like the ancient murrelets, but their young are altricial—born helpless —and must remain in the burrow for six weeks or so after hatching. Since this period of extended care takes place in the burrow rather than at sea, puffins can find their offspring simply by finding their own burrows —a visual task. Vocal recognition is not needed, and so has faded away. In fact, recognition of all types has apparently faded away. Puffins do not seem able to recognize their own offspring by any means, and will feed whoever happens to be in the burrow. They do seem able to recognize their mates, but they appear to use a combination of visual and tactile signals, rather than vocal signals, for this recognition. Although puffins do have voices, they do not often use them. After the raucous squabble of a murre colony or a penguin

rookery, a colony of puffins always seems eerily silent.

All this is not meant to suggest that penguins and auks (other than the puffins) do not use visual signals. They do. It is just that nearly all of their large repertoire of visual displays is directed to the colony at large rather than to any particular individual— and those that are individually directed usually have an accompanying aural or tactile display that is as important, or more important, than the more obvious visuals. Courtship and pair-bonding activities provide a case in point. These run the gamut from the entirely visual to the entirely tactile or aural. The purely visual displays can generally be classed as nondirective—aimed at members of the opposite sex in general—while the aural and tactile actions are generally highly directive, aimed at a specific bird—the mate —alone.

The *advertising walk* of the king penguin,

for example, is completely visual. The male bird will choose a likely-looking female (any likely-looking female), turn his back to her, and strut away, swiveling his head from side to side as he walks so that the female can see the bright-colored auricular patches on either side of his head. If the female is sufficiently impressed, she follows him, and the beginnings of a pair have been established.

Billing, on the other hand—as practiced by almost all alcid and spheniscid species—is completely tactile, and takes place almost exclusively within already mated pairs. One bird (the "active" biller) will stroke the other bird's bill with its own, an activity that apparently gives a great deal of sensual pleasure to both. Puffins, as might be expected from their large and gaudy bills, are particularly keen on billing: the passive biller will move its head around like a cat being stroked to give the active biller better access, and both birds may pirouette in place, apparently out of pure pleasure. Billing is probably directly comparable to

A king penguin in the Falkland Islands uses its bill to stroke its mate's head. Courtship activities among kings are strongly focused on the bright orange auricular patches behind the ears.

Billing—the avian equivalent of kissing—is especially avidly practiced among the puffins. These horned puffins' large, gaudy bill coverings are part of their courtship plumage, and will be shed at the end of the mating season.

Below: The ecstatic display is not limited to penguins and alcids, but is found among most seabirds. Chinstrap penguin, Nelson Island, Antarctic Peninsula.

human kissing—and like human kissing, seems to take place most strongly between recently bonded couples, with those who have been mated for a long time practicing it perfunctorily or not at all.

Between billing and the advertising walk in character are the *ecstatic displays*. As practiced by most auks and penguins—and by many other seabirds as well—ecstatic displays consist of throwing the head back, stretching the neck and wings out, and quivering in apparent ecstasy, accompanied by loud cries. There is clearly a strong visual component here, but there is a strong vocal component as well; in many cases, perhaps most, there is also a strong tactile component, as a bird and its mate engage in mutual ecstatic displays, either face-to-face with their necks and beaks touching or side by side with their wings against each other. The tactile portion of the display is for the engaged birds alone, but the vocal and visual portions are at least partly for the rest of the colony as well. This has been clearly demonstrated in experiments with little blue penguins. Ecstatic mutual displays and other forms of sexual mutual displays tend to spread through a little blue rookery in waves, with the sight and sound of couples

Side-by-side mutual ecstatic displays are common as pair-bonding rituals among most seabirds. King penguins, South Georgia Island.

engaged in them setting their neighbors to the same activities, up to and including copulation—clearly an advantage from an evolutionary standpoint, since it means that all the young in a given colony will hatch at about the same time. Both the visual and vocal displays will set off this copycat behavior, but the vocal portion seems to be the most important. Tape-recorded sounds of little blue sexual mutual displays broadcast near a little blue rookery will almost always set off a round of displaying and copulation. Tape-recorded sounds of other penguin species engaged in the same activities will have little or no effect.

Territorial displays engaged in by these birds, on the other hand, are often completely visual. Take, for example, the *slender walk,* which reaches its most highly developed form among the Adélie penguins. Adélie colonies are roughly circular, and a bird whose nest is on the landward side must necessarily thread its way through and around a number of its colony mates' closely spaced nests on its way to and from the sea.

Like all birds, these Galápagos penguins copulate from the rear.

While passing through these "foreign" portions of the colony, a bird will usually assume a highly submissive posture, head and tail lowered, shoulders hunched, feathers flattened so that the whole body looks smaller than usual, as if the bird were trying to avoid being seen altogether. Almost all penguin species, and most alcids, practice some form of the slender walk, which is an obvious adaptation to a colonial way of life. Among the alcids, the most interesting variation is probably that practiced by the puffins. Away from their own burrows they practice the slender walk in a form almost as pure as that of the Adélies, but as they get closer and closer to their own territory the walk begins to transform until, on the final approach to their own burrows, it becomes a *pelican walk,* high-stepping and strutting, head and body proudly erect. Upon reaching the burrow, the bird may continue strutting in place for several seconds. *"I'm ba-a-ad, dude. Don't mess with my turf."*

of those birds that had bred previously returned to the nesting site they had used the year before—and most of the others chose sites within four meters (about 12 feet) of their earlier nests. The correlation is high enough that many scientists suspect that mate fidelity in most of these birds may actually be nest-site fidelity; the pair bond is automatically reestablished with the same partner when both return to the same nest site to breed. (However, it is also known from studies of banded birds that if one partner is a few days late returning to the nest, the other bird may temporarily take up with a new partner, abandoning him or her when the previous mate finally shows up. The odds of this happening are not predictable one way or the other. The subject is obviously far from closed.)

Though nest-site fidelity decreases competition, it does not eliminate it entirely. This is due largely to the constantly changing demographics within the colony. Many birds will have died during the winter dispersal; others will die during the breeding

Most nonburrowing penguins and alcids lay their eggs on the bare ground, but some will prepare a small hollow, or scrape, and line it with grasses and other plants. Gentoo penguin, South Georgia Island.

Adélie penguins build nesting platforms of pebbles to raise their eggs and young above the meltwaters from the Antarctic ice. Pebble thievery is common.

Territorial behavior is at its highest during the spring, as the breeding colonies are reoccupied. (Neither penguins nor auks are as a rule strongly migratory birds, but they do disperse over the seas in the winter, often to warmer waters than those they breed near.) At about the time of the spring equinox—earlier for some species, later for others—those birds that have reached breeding age, generally three to four years, begin to feel the ancient urge to return to the breeding places and launch the new generation, and one by one they begin trickling back. Mates are greeted, and pair bonds reestablished, with much billing and allopreening. Although most of these birds mate for life, the mated couples do not normally spend their winters together.

Experienced breeders usually attempt to return to the same site they have used in previous years, a strategy that significantly reduces territorial disputes. In one study of Adélie penguins, all but about 1.5 percent

Murres rarely even prepare a scrape for their eggs, which are laid and tended on the small rock ledges of their cliffside homes.

complete nest. Most penguins and auks are content to lay their eggs directly on the ground, either in the open or in a burrow, though a shallow scrape may be prepared if no natural hollow exists, or a few pebbles may be pushed together to keep the birds' eggs from rolling away. Adélies, however—in common with their closest northern counterparts, the dovekies—build actual nests—piles or platforms of pebbles with the tops hollowed out to hold the eggs and the incubating birds. Nest building is a necessary survival tactic in these rookeries, which are at the edge of retreating snow and ice fields and are constantly coursed through by meltwaters, so that chicks not in elevated nests are likely to drown. It is also difficult. With so much of the surrounding territory covered by snow, pebbles of the right size are in constant short supply. In a large rookery, the only place an Adélie can usually obtain nest-building pebbles is other birds' nests.

Thievery has thus become well established as a necessary part of the Adélies' daily life. The birds are constantly stealing pebbles from each other. Unoccupied nests are rapidly demolished; stones may also be filched from occupied ones, although this is obviously riskier, and the thief may be chased angrily through the colony by the stone's former owner. (Sometimes other birds will join in the chase—those that aren't are taking advantage of the combatants' absence to lift a few more stones out of both of their nests.) As an experiment, an ornithologist once painted several pebbles in bright, conspicuous colors and left them in a small pile at the edge of an Adélie colony. Within a few days the pebbles had been equally distributed throughout the colony, and were being shifted from nest to nest almost on an hourly basis.

Pebbles figure in the Adélies' courtship and pair-bonding activities, too. Their rarity and value makes them highly prized items, rather like jewelry, and they are often presented as gifts by a male bird to his intended mate, or by the foraging partner to the in-

season itself, usually in the jaws of predators during foraging trips. Lurking around the outside of the colony, waiting to commandeer the nesting sites left vacant by these deaths, is a good-size population of bachelors of both sexes, consisting primarily of first-year breeders and birds that have lost their mates. This bachelor flock forms a reservoir from which vacancies within the colony can be filled, and there is a great deal of territorial conflict, indeed, as the infilling takes place and the new dynamic of the colony is established.

And some territorial disputes take place anyway, even among well-established nesters. This is especially true among the Adélies, which are one of the few species in either family to build a genuine, relatively cubating partner on his or her return to the nest for the changing of the guard. Since Adélies have trouble telling each other apart by sight, this gift-giving can sometimes lead to comically unexpected results. A returning bird may drop its stone in front of the wrong partner, bringing an angry attack by the recipient on the surprised donor. Even more embarrassing, a courting male will sometimes try to present a pebble to another male—a mistake which is likely to lead to an angry chase through the colony.

In common with most other birds, nearly all alcids and spheniscids have one family per year, nesting in the spring and raising their offspring over the summer (March through August for the auks, September through February for the Southern Hemisphere penguins). The *Aptenodytes* penguins, however—the kings and emperors—do not function this way. The larger the bird, the longer the breeding cycle, and

A pair of infant Adélie chicks are fed regurgitated krill from the parent bird's crop.

these birds are so large that gestation and chick-rearing cannot be compressed into a single season. Breeding behavior must adapt to this, or the chicks will be lost.

Each of the two species has chosen a different, though equally unusual, means of dealing with this problem. The kings have lengthened their breeding cycle to fifteen months, so that a pair of birds will breed early in the season one year, late in the season the next, and not at all in the third year. This means that all king chicks must pass at least one, and possibly two, winters in the creche stage. The emperors have avoided this problem and have kept their breeding cycle down to a single year, but at a considerable cost. In order to provide enough time for chick-rearing, they breed, lay eggs, and incubate—not in the spring and summer—but in the depths of the Antarctic winter.

The emperor breeding cycle is one of the most striking phenomena in nature. Beginning in March, as the southern days dwindle down toward the perpetual night of winter, the big birds emerge from the ocean onto the enlarging ice shelves around the

A doting emperor penguin adult cuddles its young. Antarctica.

The king penguin's breeding cycle is fifteen months long and follows a staggered three-year pattern. A given pair of birds will breed in the spring one year, in the fall the next year, and not at all in the third year.

Antarctic continent and head south, toward the rocks of the shoreline, as much as 100 kilometers (60 miles) or more from open water. Traveling principally by tobogganing—flopping on their bellies and pushing themselves along the ice with their wings— they cover the distance rapidly, and in a week or two arrive at one of the traditional rookery sites, usually on fast sea ice in the lee of a rock cliff or at the base of the great seaward wall of one of the major ice shelves. Here the ritual of courtship and mating takes place. It is an abbreviated ritual; there is no time to lose, and no energy to waste on territorial battles or on ecstatic displays. The eggs are laid in May with the anxious males attending. As soon as they are deposited on the ice, the males, with the females' assistance, roll them onto their feet and drop their brooding pouches—those large, thick folds of densely feathered skin—over them. The females then leave for the long trek back to the open sea, to forage and regain their strength. The males stay behind. They will remain there with the eggs

on their feet, barely moving, never eating— they have not, in fact, eaten since leaving the sea—for the next two months.

It is a dark, desperately cold two months. Temperatures may drop to as low as $-32°C$ ($-90°F$): winds may top 100 miles per hour. The sun never appears. The birds endure, huddling together for warmth. Survival in these conditions has required a total suppression of territoriality. Where other birds would be jabbing at one another with their beaks, making sure that a minimal personal space was kept around them, the emperors crowd together in a compact mass, and the only jostling that goes on is the constant attempt by those on the outside of the group to get into the warmer and more protected center of the huddle.

The chicks hatch in July, breaking out of the eggs while they are still on their fathers' feet in the brooding pouches. The shell fragments are pushed out of the pouches, and the chicks poke their heads out into the winter darkness. Weather conditions are like those of northern Greenland in January,

Because of the long time they take to mature, all king penguin chicks must spend at least one winter in the creche stage. These king chicks on South Georgia are about a year old.

Opposite: King penguin chicks like this one on South Georgia Island are extremely well cared for by their parents.

Pair-bonding among Adélies is reaffirmed each time a foraging parent returns to the nest.

A group of kings prepares to go to sea at the edge of a rock-strewn beach on South Georgia.

but colder; fortunately, the chicks are prepared for this, with thick coats of infant down and an odd, distinctive pattern of facial markings—a black stripe down the center of the head set off by large white circles around the eyes—that appears to function as a visual target, allowing the parent birds to locate their offspring by starlight if nothing else is available. Like all babies, the chicks are immediately hungry; if the mothers have not returned (the usual situation), the fathers must manage somehow. The fathers do this by secreting a thick, milklike substance known as *penguin milk* from the linings of their crops and regurgitating it to feed the chicks—a remarkable feat, considering that the fathers have very likely had no food themselves for the past three months.

Eventually the mothers rejoin their families, tobogganing in from the coast, and take over the feeding and baby-sitting chores. The fathers, who by this time have lost a third or more of their body weight,

are finally able to rest, recuperate, and take their turn in the sea to forage and regain their strength.

In case anyone reading this book still thinks of penguin and auk behavior as totally stereotyped and instinctive, I would like to close this chapter with two more anecdotal accounts.

The first is well documented in scientific literature: it concerns an Adélie penguin that was seen by researchers to return to its nest after losing a territorial dispute with a neighbor and, apparently still angry, beat its own chick to death. This is not the behavior of an instinct-shackled organism. Instinct may explain both territoriality and normal parenting, but it is difficult to extend that explanation to child abuse. And on a more upbeat note, all of Gary Ballew's alcids in the Seattle Aquarium—birds that "instinctively" catch live prey beneath the water and bring it to the surface to consume it—not only eat dead fish and krill (all captive sea-

birds must learn to do that, or starve) but consume it underwater, swallowing one "prey" while reaching for the next.

The reason for the Seattle alcids' behavior is probably straightforward enough. Since the birds are only fed once a day, they must maximize their food intake during this single brief session; and since they are in competition with their exhibit mates, maximization means grabbing as much as possible during each foraging run, which in turn means swallowing each piece as you grab it to get it out of the way so you can grab another. Nothing unreasonable about that, of course, but that is precisely the point. The thing that amazes observers of this behavior is not that it is unreasonable, but the opposite: that it is so very, very reasonable. Birds are not supposed to reason. What does this say about the primacy of instinct and the inflexibility of behavior associated with basic drives? Perhaps the strongest message is this: birds are not the only ones who cling inflexibly to fixed mental patterns. Scientists can do it, too.

Gentoo penguins and whale vertebrae, Port Lockroy, Antarctic Peninsula.

The pale light of an
Antarctic dawn awakens
sleeping Adélies on ice
floes off the coast of the
Antarctic Peninsula.

7
WADDLING TOWARD
ARMAGEDDON?

The fragile bones of birds do not fossilize easily, so it is difficult to establish lines of phylogenetic descent from direct evidence. It is known, however, that both auks and penguins originated in the middle to late Miocene era, about 65 million years ago, and that for both families, the species mix then was almost completely unlike what it is today. The principal difference was size. Miocene penguins and auks averaged much larger than those found in our own seas. Fossil beds in New Zealand and on Seymour Island, near the tip of Antarctica's Palmer Peninsula, have yielded the tarsi of penguins that probably stood nearly six feet tall and weighed in at over 300 pounds. California beds hold the remains of a group of big, flightless Miocene auks known as mancallines, which, while not as large as most living penguins, were larger than any living alcid.

Why are today's penguins and auks smaller than those of the Miocene? Why did the largest species in both familes become extinct? Scientists do not know, but they have come up with a plausible speculation. They believe that the large wing-propelled divers became extinct because they could not handle competition from the cetaceans and pinnipeds—the seagoing mammals. The evidence is circumstantial, but it is strong. The decline of the large diving birds corresponds almost precisely with the rise of the aquatic mammals. And those alcid and spheniscid species that have survived—with the possible exception of the emperor penguins—are small enough that they take a different portion of the prey spectrum than that taken by their mammalian competitors. Gause's Principle is real: niche competition is fatal, and mammals have caused—either directly or indirectly, the dis-

Opposite: This gentoo chick on South Georgia will need all the protection its affectionate parent can give it.

187

The bones of birds do not fossilize as easily as those of other vertebrates, so scientists have less information about their origins. Gentoo penguins and whale bones, Port Lockroy, Antarctic Peninsula.

tinction is immaterial—the extinction of most of these vanished species of birds.

We are mammals, too. This point should not entirely escape our attention.

As we approach the twenty-first century, many populations—and some whole species—of penguins and auks do not appear to be approaching it with us. In most cases, our own activities—[directly or indirectly, the distinction is again immaterial]—are the principal cause of these imminent extinctions. None of the current declines can be declared absolutely irreversible, and no actual extinction has taken place in these families since that of the great auk in 1844. Some species—notably the chinstrap penguin and the horned puffin—actually appear to be extending their ranges. But the overall trend is drastically downward, and the outlook for all of these birds is grim.

On March 24, 1989, in what has become one of the most widely publicized environmental disasters of modern times, the super-

tanker *Exxon Valdez* ran aground on Bligh Reef in the northeast corner of Alaska's Prince William Sound, rupturing her hull and spilling somewhere around 11 million gallons of crude oil into the cold northern waters. Twelve hundred miles of shoreline were eventually fouled by the spreading slick—a distance roughly equivalent to that of the Atlantic shore from Cape Cod to Cape Hatteras, or the Pacific from San Francisco to northern Vancouver Island. More than 100,000 birds died. Most of these were alcids.

The primary victims were murres, which were rafting in the area in preparation for the breeding season. Some of these birds became so oil-coated that they simple sank, and thus drowned. Others were poisoned by the large quantities of oil they ingested in an effort to preen it off their bodies. Most, however, succumbed to hypothermia, that is, they froze to death. When oil coats a bird's feathers, the feathers lose the ability to cling to one another, and the tiny pockets of air that give them their insulating ability are opened up and destroyed. Cold penetrates to the bird's body, metabolic heat escapes, and the bird dies.

None of this was new to the scientists studying the *Exxon Valdez* disaster; most of them had seen it many times before. The litany of major oil spills at sea is a long one, and each has killed large numbers of seabirds, which are among the creatures most vulnerable to their effects. There was the breakup of the *Torrey Canyon* off the Land's End peninsula at the western tip of Cornwall, Great Britain, in 1967; the grounding of the *Metula* in the Strait of Magellan in August 1974 (the middle of the Southern Hemisphere winter); the wreck of the *Amoco Cadiz* off the coast of Brittany in April 1978; and the long series of shipping disasters off Africa's Cape of Good Hope (four major spills and a number of minor ones occurred in these waters during one notorious three-month period in the spring of 1968; there have been many others before and since). Ominously, the area subject to spills has recently been extended to the fragile coast of Antarctica itself. Two ships, the *Bahía Paraiso* and the *Humboldt,* ran aground off the Palmer Peninsula within a few weeks of each other in January 1989. Neither was a tanker, but the fuel oil spilled in each case was substantial enough: both incidents took place near Adélie rookeries. Hundreds—probably thousands—of birds were killed.

As most oil-pollution authorities will tell you, however, the major problem is not the large, headline-grabbing spills and the inevitable well-meaning but destructive cleanup attempts that follow (often referred to by those who must deal with their effects as "the second spill"). The real culprits are not the big spills but the thousands of little ones. Ships discharge oily ballast, or spill fuel while loading it, or trail diesel oil behind from leaks in their engine casings. Oil filled too close to the top of a tank in cool weather will expand as it warms, overflowing into the ocean. Since 1975 it has been against international law to pump out bal-

last tanks at sea, but there are times it must be done anyway, because the ballast has become too full, and the ship will founder if the oil is not pumped. Nobody pays much attention to international law, anyhow. The result of the multitude of these daily "incidents" (as opposed to "accidents") is the discharge of many millions of gallons into the world's oceans every year, much of it near seabird rookeries, which tend to cluster near rocks and shallow waters where fish production is highest and sailing is the most treacherous. Oil pollution, mostly of the leak-a-day kind, has been blamed for the virtual disappearance of breeding colonies of puffins and murres in France and their decline in England, and is probably the largest factor in the decimation of the jackass pen-

Chinstrap penguins are among the few members of either the penguin or alcid families that are currently extending their range.

guin populations of South Africa, which have plummeted from several million birds at the close of World War II to fewer than 100,000—some authorities say fewer than 50,000—today.

Oil pollution is the most obvious human-caused destroyer of seabirds, but it is not the only one. Take plastic, for instance. An estimated 450,000 plastic containers are tossed overboard from the world's merchant shipping fleet daily. Broken up but not chemically changed by wave action, these form into small plastic bits that literally carpet the seas. Birds eat them, either directly in the mistaken belief that they are prey or indirectly through the consumption of fish that have fed on them, and now carry plastic-lined digestive tracts. Since these plastic bits cannot be digested, they become concentrated in the birds' crops, from which they will later be regurgitated to feed the young. This means that the young birds'

diets are even higher in plastics than those of their parents. Sometimes this kills the chicks outright, but a more common effect is to slowly starve them owing to the high proportion of "food" with no nutritive value. The plastics problem is so widespread that scientists have actually begun to monitor ocean pollution patterns by studying the regurgitated crop contents of petrels and other surface-feeding birds. Penguins and auks, which feed at depth, are probably not quite so strongly affected, but no one knows for certain.

Commercial fishing is another hazard faced by these birds in their struggle for survival. Here, competition for prey is the principal factor. Though humans are no match for penguins and auks when it comes to catching individual fish, our methods of mass prey capture are far in advance of those of the birds, so our total catch is much greater than theirs. Competition with the huge anchovy fishery off Peru is probably one of the chief causes of the decline of the

Plastic debris accidentally swallowed by seabirds becomes concentrated in their crops and then is fed to the young. These sometimes develop symptoms of malnutrition owing to the high proportion of indigestible matter from which they can derive no nutritive value. Gentoo penguins, South Georgia Island.

Humboldt penguin, whose population has fallen to between 5,000 and 8,000 birds during the last decade. The extremely similar jackass penguin is probably also suffering from fisheries competition, along with its problems with oil pollution.

In the Northern Hemisphere, fisheries competition has not historically been a major factor. Most of the auks feed principally on plankton or krill, and those that do not are likely to take fish that humans don't want. Lately, however, commercial fishermen have begun to target some of these "trash" species as populations of the more attractive fish have declined. One of these newly exploited species is the sand eel—a chief prey of the Atlantic puffin. It is still too early to tell what the effects of this human niche redirection are likely to be on puffin populations, but they cannot be beneficial.

Worse yet are attempts to take humans lower on the food chain by harvesting krill. Fortunately, krill seem almost unpalatably bland to human taste buds. Despite relatively large-scale ventures launched by both the Japanese and the Russians, they have yet to become a marketable commodity. Massive exploitation of this resource could still happen, however, as human populations increase and other ocean species decline. The prospective impact on the pygoscelid penguins, which are almost totally dependent on krill, is a concern to scientists.

A secondary problem caused by commercial fishing, but one that needs to be mentioned, is the toll taken on alcids by drift nets. These immense nets of nearly invisible monofilament line may be 150 to 200 meters (500 to 660 feet) tall and several miles in length. They are sometimes called *gill nets* because they are designed to trap fish by the gills as they try to swim through them. Unfortunately, they also entangle diving birds and mammals, which then drown because they cannot resurface for air. Murres are the most common victims because of the depths the nets are normally set at—roughly 50

Chinstrap penguins give a buried oil drum a wide berth on Deception Island. Even in the Antarctic, oil pollution is responsible for significant numbers of seabird deaths.

In the Northern Hemisphere, burrowing alcids such as this tufted puffin are threatened by overgrazing, which increases the erosion rate of the soil their burrows are excavated in.

A Magellanic peers from its burrow on Cape Horn. Burrowing penguins are threatened with the destruction of their habitat by guano miners, who quarry away the birds' homes.

meters (140 to 170 feet) below the surface —but puffins, murrelets, razorbills, and indeed virtually all species of alcids have been impacted to some extent. The problem is not small. One study in the Davis Strait off western Greenland, where the nets were set to take salmon, found that the rate of capture of murres was actually greater than that of the salmon—500,000 to 750,000 per year. Declines of 50 to 70 percent in the breeding populations of murres on California's Farallon Islands during the 1970s and 1980s have been statistically linked to a six-fold increase in drift-net fishing over the same period. And a 1984 report from British Columbia noted that some 200 marbled murrelets were being caught annually in drift nets set in Barclay sound, on the west coast of Vancouver Island—a number that does not seem large until you realize that there were only about 2,000 marbled murrelets there to begin with. Each year's kill thus represented 10 percent of the breeding population. Perhaps the birds can withstand an additional attrition rate of that magnitude, but with a population that small already it is not an experiment that one wants to see carried to its conclusion.

Direct predation on the birds by humans and the animals they have introduced has historically been significant. It was the cause of the extinction of the great auk, but it does not seem to be much of a factor today, though a canning factory specializing in murre meat was still operating in Greenland as recently as 1987, and subsistence hunting for auks and penguins, including egg gathering, continues to be a part of human cultures in such widely separated areas as Scandinavia and the Falkland Islands. The birds are no longer boiled down commercially for their oil, and the practice of farming Arctic foxes for their fur by placing them on inaccessible islands off the coast of Alaska, where they had free run of the previously predator-free seabird colonies, is now illegal. The greatest continuing impact from direct human-caused predation is probably on Iceland, where North American mink imported for fur farming have escaped and are increasing at the expense of auk eggs, but even this is relatively small. A larger problem is indirect human-caused predation by gulls, whose populations have greatly increased during recent decades because of their ability to winter off human garbage dumps. Gulls are the chief natural predators on alcid colonies. Thus has been formed the curious but very real correlation between our current solid-waste-disposal crisis and the decline of auk populations in nearly all populated areas of the Northern Hemisphere. Everything is connected to everything else. John Muir was right.

The biggest threat to both auks and penguins, however, is not predation, or competition, or accidental entrapment, or even

Overleaf: Atlantic puffins on their burrowing grounds at Witless Bay, Newfoundland.

A trio of Magellanic penguin chicks demands a handout from a startled parent on Argentina's Valdés Peninsula.

pollution. It is the destruction of their habitat. The birds are losing their places to live, and that is a far greater hazard to the viability of a species than the destruction of its individual members, even in large numbers, can ever be.

Birds can rebound from predation by increasing their birthrates and by recruiting new breeding pairs from the nonbreeding population that hangs around the edges of any good-size colony. They can deal with competition—at least to a certain extent—by going after alternate prey. But they cannot breed without breeding sites. Alternatives are normally not feasible, though the bird may try. There is always a reason why a bird breeds where it does. Almost always it has to do with maximizing the survival of the hatchlings. Alternatives are always less satisfactory, and are often downright hazardous.

The examples, unfortunately, are multitudinous. All *Spheniscus* penguins, for instance, breed in burrows. Wherever possible these will be dug in soil; but soil is at a premium on most of the rocky islands these birds inhabit, so they have turned as an alternative to digging burrows in guano deposits, their own and those of the ever-present gulls and pelicans. It is a method that has worked well for millennia (intact 10,000-year-old penguin eggs have been found in guano in Peru), but it cannot contend with human miners, who strip the islands of their guano for the phosphates it contains, literally carting away the birds' homes. The problem has stabilized somewhat lately. Guano miners today in most nations may not legally take away any more than has been laid down by the birds in the course of a year. But the stabilization has occurred at levels considerably below those that the birds have historically had access to, and as a consequence the colonies have shrunk. Some South African penguins have attempted to nest in the open, without a great deal of success. For a species already reeling from the blows of oil pollution and

King penguins ignore a cruise ship in the harbor at South Georgia Island. Tourism is becoming a significant threat to wildlife in both the Antarctic and the high Arctic.

fisheries competition, this habitat loss may be fatal.

A similar problem is faced by the tufted puffin and the rhinoceros auklet in western North America. These are also burrowing species, constructing their burrows in the soil at the edges of seaside bluffs and on the summits of sea stacks. This soil has historically been well anchored by grass, but the introduction of grazing livestock (and in some areas the prolific European rabbit) has taken care of that. With the grass gone down these introduced gullets, soil erosion has intensified, washing the birds' homes over the cliffs and out to sea. This has forced the puffins and auklets to concentrate their burrow construction in the few places the rabbits and livestock haven't been able to reach, and these spots have become so thoroughly riddled with the birds' tunnels that the soil surface is collapsing, so that erosion here, too, is increased. The problem continues to compound itself; its full effects have probably yet to be felt.

The most seriously threatened of these birds, though—and among the most threatened of all birds anywhere—are the three species that utilize breeding sites in old-growth forest: the yellow-eyed penguin, the marbled murrelet, and the ancient murrelet. The yellow-eyed penguin and the ancient murrelet nest in burrows dug in the duff at the bases of the great old trees: the marbled murrelets actually nest in the trees, laying their eggs on platforms constructed of moss in the crotches of main limbs some distance up the trunks of giant conifers such as Douglas firs or redwoods. As the old-growth forests fall to the ax, these birds fall, too. The most seriously endangered is the yellow-eyed; it is currently clinging precariously to a few offshore islands and to one single half-mile-long stretch of old growth along the shore of New Zealand's South Island. The population is under 2,000 pairs, and the long-term outlook is extremely grim.

This has been a rather depressing chapter, so perhaps we should end it on an upbeat note. Though their species as a whole is in trouble, there is one breeding colony of Humboldt penguins that is doing very well indeed—not in Peru, where these birds normally live, but on Mission Bay in downtown San Diego, California.

The Mission Bay Humboldts are a project of San Diego Sea World, but they are not an exhibit. Their enclosure is on a part of the grounds that is quarantined from the public. Unlike the other birds in Sea World's highly successful breeding program, the Humboldts are not being bred for exhibit but as a hedge against declining wild populations. Half-in and half-out of the bay—so that the birds have full access to the water—the roomy enclosure includes a large earthen bank in which to construct burrows, plenty of lounging room, and a good pull-out beach. The penguins are apparently thriving. "We're getting two breeding seasons a year," says Sea World staffer Melissa Barringer happily. One breeding season corresponds with the normal Southern Hemisphere breeding time; the other takes place six months later, in the Northern Hemisphere summer. This bimodal breeding pattern means that the colony's numbers are increasing rapidly, a fact that gives ornithologists much hope. The Humboldt penguin is one of the most endangered of the world's birds. If the wild Humboldts should disappear entirely, they could be reintroduced from San Diego.

We share our world with these delightful birds. Sometimes we do not share it very well. As the San Diego project proves, however, we are capable of making up for that. We need not watch helplessly as they waddle toward Armageddon. We can intervene. And the cold, rich waters of the southern and northern seas can continue to throng with the graceful flights of these birds that swim with their wings, treating the deep green space of the water like the blue space of the air.

Opposite: Two chinstraps on Nelson Island appear to contemplate their future in an increasingly human-modified world.

Overleaf: A mixed flock of kings and gentoos gathers on the edge of an icy pool on South Georgia Island.

Chinstraps, Nelson
Island, Antarctica.

INDEX